GEISHA

*A Unique World
of Tradition,
Elegance, and Art*

John Gallagher

PRC

Produced in 2003 by
PRC Publishing Ltd,
The Chrysalis Building
Bramley Road, London W10 6SP

A member of **Chrysalis** Books plc

This edition published 2003
Distributed in the U.S. and Canada by:
Sterling Publishing Co., Inc.
387 Park Avenue South
New York, NY 10016

ISBN 1 85648 697 4

Printed and bound in China

NOTE:
Japanese names in the main text are written in Japanese style—family name first,
given name second. The value of the Yen has fluctuated greatly in the past. An
average worker earns between three and five million Yen annually.

CONTENTS

INTRODUCTION

the flower-and-willow world

Top-class geisha are

living embodiments of iki.

Right: The Japanese cityscape is an unlikely arena for a two-hundred-and-fifty-year-old tradition of ultra-aesthetic entertainment.

Far right: Two geisha walk along a Kyoto alleyway. On the left of this rather run down street is a *mah-jong* parlor.

…the perfect type of a perfect pleasure. It is exquisite, and leaves one unsatisfied. What more could one want?

Oscar Wilde, *The Picture of Dorian Gray*

Deep in the urban sprawl of modern Japanese cities lie the hanamachi, or "flower towns." Amid the traffic, neon, and concrete, these clusters of narrow lanes and traditional wooden townhouses are a world apart, elegant and understated, like still rock pools in a concrete jungle. The hanamachi are home to a way of life very different to the world outside. Their culture is an intricate, dynamic human ecosystem of craftsmen and artists, with dense networks of relationships governed by painstaking etiquette. And all for one aim: the celebration of the artistic and physical beauty of highly-trained female performers. For above all, the hanamachi are home to one of Japan's most famous yet enigmatic symbols: the geisha.

The word "geisha" is composed of two parts—*gei* and *sha*, "-sha" being simply a suffix along the lines of "-ist" or "-ician" in English. *Gei* is a common word with a wide range of meanings covering arts, crafts, and accomplishments. In everyday life—at, say, a company drinking party—one will often hear a modest Japanese calling himself a "person without *gei*" (*gei no nai hito*). In other words, this person does not have (or at least pretends not to have) a party piece, and so is no good at entertaining people. In essence, this is what geisha do: they entertain people. They are the crème de la crème of Japanese entertainers. Their clients are drawn mainly from the top of Japan's many hierarchies. They pay small, and sometimes not so small, fortunes for their entertainment.

The reason for this is twofold. Firstly, geisha are highly trained professionals in the fields of traditional Japanese dance, music, and tea

The hanamachi are home to a way of life very different to the world outside.

ceremony. Their expertise also covers traditional games and poetry. Most crucially of all, they command in full the etiquette, deportment, and repartee which form a very special Japanese aesthetic called *iki*. Ultra-aesthetic but playful and witty, *iki* refers to a highly cultivated but not solemn sensibility, as open to broad jokes and puns as it is deeply versed in traditional high arts. Top-class geisha are living embodiments of *iki*. The clients of top-class geisha are expected to share this sensibility too; in men, it's called *tsu*. It can be translated as urbaneness with some loss of depth. The *iki/tsu* sensibility resists set rules as that would be quite un-*iki* (*buiki*)—vulgar and uncouth.

All geisha work to entertain their guests, who are usually but not always men, and entertaining does not just mean offering some form of educational culture. Nevertheless, in engaging the services of a qualified geisha, the clientele are hiring an elite professional, who is as thoroughly trained as a medical consultant. They expect to pay accordingly. The commitment to training is at the core of a geisha's professionalism. Traditionally, training started early at six years of age. Now, it generally starts at fifteen or later. After this point, geisha—especially those of the elite hanamachi—literally never stop training. Even at sixty years of age and over, they continue to polish their mastery of the arts, especially dance.

A second reason for the expense of hiring geisha lies in their costume. A single kimono is a one-of-a-kind, handmade work of art costing at least 150,000 Yen and anything up to 7,000,000 Yen. Geisha at the top of their

Left: Apprentice Kyoto geisha, or maiko, learn their trade at traditional schools. Kyoto and Tokyo are the main modern centers of geisha culture. Maiko are very distinctive in appearance, with their long, trailing hairpins and highly decorated kimonos.

profession may go through literally dozens a year. Each requires an *obi*, or sash, at a similar price or higher, along with wigs or hair ornaments that are changed every month and cost the same again. Geisha sit at the center of a dizzying network of crafts and skills, from specialist textile workers to calligraphers to sake warmers. The money to pay them all comes from the client. This does not include hire of the party venue, food, or drinks which are all added separately to his bill. An evening at a Japanese hostess bar is like hiring a low-budget small car for a day trip to an amusement park. But ordering a geisha party is like arranging for a hand-gilded eighteenth-century carriage, with liveried footmen, to convey the passenger, in solemn procession, to a formal but lively banquet at a medieval guildhall.

The key institutions of the hanamachi are the *okiya* and the *ochaya. Okiya* are geisha houses, where the performers live as a family, either natural or adoptive. Each *okiya* will normally have one or two fully-fledged geisha and one or two trainees. The house is governed by a

Right: Geisha walking along a Kyoto street. In many ways, their world functions as a kind of time machine. The common English phrase "geisha girl" is quite misleading. These professionals may carry on into their 60s or later.

Mother or Grandmother, who is referred to by that title by the geisha. There are also a number of live-in maids. No men live in geisha houses. Indeed, with a few rare exceptions, men are not normally permitted past the entrance chamber. Apart from providing dwelling space, *okiya* are storehouses of the extremely precious costumes and accessories geisha need to perform their work. Kyoto *okiya* are relatively simple, not very large, traditional Japanese townhouses, floored with tatami matting, as is normal in all traditional living spaces. These are thick blocks of tightly woven straw, bound with cloth at the edges. Their particular cut-grass fragrance is familiar to anyone in Japan. The word *okiya* (literally, "house of placement") is used in Kyoto; in Edo geisha dwellings were simply called *geisha-ya*—geisha houses.

Ochaya (literally, "teahouses") are where geisha perform at private parties. Actually, teahouse gives a rather inaccurate impression of these establishments. Though they began as simple, informal restaurants catering to pilgrims and other travelers, they gradually

Left: A Japanese woman dressed in traditional kimono, in Kyoto. Kimono use as a part of everyday life is in rapid decline. The art of putting them on has died out in many families.

Right: A geisha serving at a table at a convention in Kyoto. Geisha are called to work in a variety of venues. For some Japanese men, the ritual of pouring drinks has a slightly erotic edge.

evolved into much more exclusive venues. *Ochaya* serve as highly prestigious function rooms, where geisha entertain small parties of guests. They are not restaurants, though they have kitchens to arrange meals provided by outside caterers. They also provide alcoholic and other drinks. Tea is not usually high on the list of customers' requests.

The best-known *ochaya*, such as Kyoto's Ichirikitei, are famous spots in Japan. They have long histories and have been the scenes of many secret meetings, plots, and assignations down the ages. They are often the setting for historical novels and dramas, which can give a rather lurid impression of what goes on inside them. In contrast to *okiya* (geisha houses), *ochaya* are quite luxurious. Their exteriors are remarkable for their determinedly low-key

elegance. They could almost be mistaken for upmarket private houses. Most *ochaya* are tucked discreetly away on back streets in the hanamachi. Colors are muted, materials are natural, and the signs are tiny scraps of elegant calligraphy. The contrast to the screaming neon and garish billboards of the modern Japanese street could not be greater. The demure look oozes exclusivity and expense.

In Japanese architecture, luxury does not mean that the rooms look startlingly different from the norm. Rather, the materials are more costly. The party rooms are no different in layout from an ordinary tavern with long, low tables on tatami matting. Seating is on cushions, or low chairs with backs but no legs. Often, several groups of geisha work at the same time, entertaining separate groups of guests. A

Left: Tourists and locals walk along a traditional street in Kyoto.

customer may slide back a paper door to peek in on a neighboring party. This is frowned upon slightly, but it often happens. If a lovesick guest trawls through the rooms in search of a favorite dancer, it can even be considered rather endearing behavior.

Geisha parties tend to baffle Westerners. Japanese dance, while graceful, is not particularly rhythmical or spectacular. The music and singing sound dissonant and jarring to an untrained ear. Even the performers themselves, gorgeously bedecked and painted as they are, are not always necessarily beauties to a Western or even to a Japanese observer. A geisha performer may in fact be in her sixties or even older. As for the geisha's conversation, it may seem perfectly banal. The humor, where it is intelligible, often consists of double entendres

at best and single entendres at worst, and it is not unknown for the humor to be directed at the foreigner in their midst. The geisha encourage party games that may seem bizarrely childish, with variations of pass-the-parcel followed by variations of scissors-paper-rock. Penalty games are common, with the loser removing a piece of clothing (if a male guest) or downing a glass of sake as punishment. Japanese corporate drinking parties feature much alcohol-induced bonhomie, backslapping, raucous laughter, and stereotyped "outrageous" behavior. For the executives, it is a way to connect with each other outside the highly stressful pressure-cooker that is Japanese office life. For the outsider, it can all get a little tedious and geisha parties are often no exception. After an hour or two of this, the party is over and the

Right: A geisha plays the shamisen while kneeling on a straw tatami mat. Learning to play the traditional instrument is an essential part of a geisha's accomplishments. A geisha party would be unimaginable without it.

geisha may already be long gone. The visitor to Japan, after the corporate farewell bows or on the way to a second, less extortionately expensive do, may well wonder—what is all the fuss over geisha about?

The ideal Japanese guest—the man of *tsu*—is looking at a very different picture. He is, first of all, relaxed and at home in a deeply familiar environment. Both geisha families and guests pride themselves on building up enduring relationships with each other that span the generations. The ideal guest may well have been introduced to the *ochaya* by his father. His birth may have been celebrated by the mothers (real or adoptive) of the geisha he is bantering with. The families who run the *ochaya* do not think of their establishments as public space. Rather, they see them as family homes where guests call and enjoy the company of geisha. Money does not change hands directly between the guest and the *ochaya* on the same evening. Bills are sent to the guest's company or home up to a month later. Trust is essential for the system to work.

The ideal guest sees the *ochaya* as a kind of second living room or club, and he goes there for his own enjoyment as well as using it for entertaining business or political clients. He is normally loyal to one *ochaya* only, and will commonly book geisha from the hanamachi it belongs to. Not only is he at home here, he is also well versed in the performances that the geisha give. He may come from a related arts background himself, kimono textile weaving or kabuki theater for example. He may be (and in Kyoto often is) a priest from a local Buddhist temple. Or he may even be a high-ranking member of the *yakuza*, or Japanese mafia. (This is an organization that prides itself on ferociously strict codes of old-world discipline not a million miles removed from the geisha world itself.) In any case, he will have strong connections with traditional Japan —not only through his personal interests but also in his background and daily life. He will be familiar with *Nihon buyo* (traditional Japanese dance) and the shamisen, the geisha musical instrument par excellence.

The shamisen is played to accompany dances in a variety of styles—*nagauta* (literally "long song"), *kouta* (little song), *hauta* (a short love song), and *jiuta* (traditional folk song, literally "song of the earth"). The dances are varied and legion, with roots in noh or kabuki drama depending on the geisha's hanamachi. They are called *The Pine Tree Tale*, *Black Hair*, *The Seasons in Kyoto*, *Cherry Blossoms at Night*, *Tale of the Vagabond Shamisen Player*, *Selling Ferns*, and *Dawn*, among a host of others.

The ideal guest is at home in an environment that he can understand. Apart from enjoying the music and dancing, he will admire with a practiced eye both the geisha and their costumes, the garden outside the window, and the *tokonoma* or alcove, with its seasonal flower arrangement and its matching scroll of calligraphy. He will appreciate how the arrangements in the room itself harmonize with the season and how the performers, in appearance and action, do the same. He is neither overawed nor boorish. He is certainly not solemn; he drinks and makes jokes with his fellow guests and the

The shamisen is played to accompany dances in a variety of styles.

performers. Above all, the ideal guest takes pleasure in the atmosphere of *iki*:

> *Iki* reveals something of the spirit of old Tokyo. Edo: refined, sophisticated, but more—sensuous, a suggestion of eroticism. The wealthy merchant classes of Edo refined the sense of *iki*, and the overtones of the elegant geisha of the pleasure districts of Edo are still a part of the meaning of *iki*…Essential to *iki* is a quality of worldliness, experience, love affairs past, a passion matured.[1]

Of course, this ideal man of *tsu* is a rare animal and getting rarer by the day. Guests at a geisha party are often politicians, deep in discussion of the factional wrangles that pass for Japanese politics. They may be baseball stars or other celebrities, with very limited knowledge of or interest in what they are seeing. They may be utterly bamboozled foreign film directors or Japanese business executives equally at sea. The geisha do their best to entertain them just the same; that is their job, after all. With the decline of the independently wealthy, leisured connoisseur, however, they face an increasingly uphill task.

The soul of the hanamachi is the *ochaya* party, known in Japanese as *ozashiki*. In normal language, *ozashiki* simply means a space with tatami mat flooring. In geisha parlance, it means both the party and the room in which it happens. Geisha learn dance and music at specialized schools. It is at *ozashiki* parties that geisha hone their essential skills as entertainers.

There are many other calls on a successful geisha's time, however. They often perform at banquets in *ryotei* (traditional *haute cuisine*

Right: The Heian shrine in Kyoto. Shinto shrines can be recognized by the distinctive *torii* gates. The geisha world is relatively religious by the not very pious standards of society as a whole.

restaurants) and hotels, entertaining groups of forty or fifty people. They sometimes travel to hanamachi in other cities for guest performances, and occasionally even perform abroad. Highly successful geisha are often asked to do publicity shots for local tourism boards, especially in Kyoto. They also appear in magazine and TV commercials.

However, the main work of the geisha, apart from private parties in the *ochaya*, is the yearly round of public dance performances and festivals at which they are expected to appear. The calendar is especially elaborate in Kyoto. This is especially true in Gion Kobu, the most elite and artistically demanding hanamachi in Japan. The Cherry Dance in April, the Gion Festival in July, and the Festival of the Ages in October are only three of the highlights of a year-long process. Rehearsals are time-consum-

ing and exacting. The performances must be flawless, because the honor of the geisha, her geisha house, and her entire hanamachi are under scrutiny. These performances bring no financial reward; in fact, taking part costs a great deal of money. The rewards are measured in exposure and, above all, prestige.

Maiko, Geiko, and *Taikomochi*

The geisha precincts (hanamachi) are collectively known as the flower-and-willow world. Flowers are traditionally symbols of the erotic and willows of gracefulness. The flower-and-willow world originated in eighteenth-century Edo and spread throughout Japan. However, its modern bastion is Kyoto, the ancient capital of Japan and the seat of its traditional arts. The most prestigious hanamachi of all are found in

Left: Wearing brightly colored kimonos, geisha perform in the Cherry Dances at a theater in the Gion district of Kyoto.

Right: By the time she becomes a fully-fledged professional, the geisha is steeped in the culture and lore of hanamachi life.

this city. Only Kyoto's Gion Kobu hanamachi, for example, is licensed to cater to visiting foreign heads of state. There, hanamachi disciplines and traditions are retained in full.

The word "geisha" itself is rarely used in the Kyoto hanamachi, however. Instead, geisha are divided into two types, maiko and geiko. Geiko are fully qualified geisha. Maiko are apprentice geisha and the term is unique to Kyoto. The Tokyo equivalent is *hangyoku* (literally "half-jewel"), a term that implied that their fees were half of a qualified geisha. Child *hangyoku*, as young as nine years old, disappeared with the outlawing of child labor in the 1950s. They now start at around fifteen years of age. Maiko, too, start their training much later in life these days, to the dismay of traditionalists who worry that a decline in skills will result.

Many other cities have large, famous hanamachi, especially Tokyo, with its rich pool of political, bureaucratic, and corporate clients. Highly-paid and qualified geisha work here, too. But Kyoto prides itself in something other cities can never have. As the font of traditional

Japanese culture, Kyoto is home to the founding schools of Japanese dance, tea ceremony, flower arranging, and calligraphy. A delicate but dynamic linkage exists between the various artistic *milieux,* in a traditional social and architectural setting like no other in Japan. In his book *Lost Japan,* the writer Alex Kerr wrote of the tea ceremony, which originated in Kyoto, as the meeting place of all Japanese traditional arts, from clothing and pottery to calligraphy and architecture. Perhaps the only element missing here is performance art. The Kyoto geiko and maiko, with their formal links through dance to the noh drama and kabuki worlds, provide this linkage. In fact, with its intimate connections to the traditional arts and the national ruling circles, the flower-and-willow world spans political, artistic, and sporting elite circles like no other comparable group in Japan.

Maiko (apprentice geisha) are one of the great sights of Kyoto tourism. They look quite different from fully qualified geisha. The maiko is the peak of traditional Japanese femininity. Her kimono collar hangs loose to highlight the nape, which is a primary erogenous zone in Japanese sexuality. Her white makeup covers the nape, with two (or sometimes three) stripes of flesh left exposed. The overall effect is to conceal, reveal, and tantalize—much like the garter belt or cleavage in Western costume. The back of her kimono hangs loose, showing a glimpse of her white-painted back, fringed by a scarlet collar. Her kimono is bright and colorful, with a spectacular *obi* tied at the back and hanging almost to her ankles. Taking tiny steps, she teeters along the street in wooden platform clogs called *okobo*, about ten centimeters high. She is a walking compendium of everything chic in traditional Japan, exaggerated to the utmost.

Maiko are apprentices, in the formal sense that they are under contract to their *okiya* or geisha house. The *okiya* supplies them with food, board, tuition fees, and most importantly, kimonos, *obi*, and the other tools of their trade. The expenses which maiko incur are considerable. They have to be repaid from earnings and repayments usually continue after the maiko becomes a fully-fledged geisha. Only when her debts are fully settled is she free to move out and live independently.

As apprentices, maiko do not have the full mastery of dance, conversation, and other arts expected of a geiko. Indeed, in many cases they are still struggling with the special dialect of Japanese used by Kyoto geisha which is much softer and more traditional than the modern standard language, which is based on the language of Tokyo. A great deal of their work, especially in the early stages, consists of attending private parties (*ozashiki*) and watching their Older Sisters (i.e. their mentors) doing their job. Indeed, one stage of the maiko's apprenticeship is called *minarai*, which means "learning by watching." The training of maiko consists of three elements. The formal arts training takes place in geisha schools, which exist in every Kyoto hanamachi. Their entertainment training is done in the various teahouses, at parties with their mentors. An equally important skill is learned on the street and in visits to other

Left: A finely dressed maiko, caught in a graceful pose with her umbrella as she walks among the spring cherry blossoms.

geisha houses and teahouses: the social skill of navigating the dense, complex social web of the hamamachi. Formal greetings on the street, exchanges of gifts and visits are important in Japan for people in all walks of life. For a maiko, they are crucial if she is to build up the support network she needs to survive and thrive in the hanamachi.

Despite being apprentices, maiko are immensely valued in the Kyoto hanamachi. Their formal debuts are spectacular events, drawing press photographers and crowds of loyal fans. A successful maiko is an enormous asset to her house, both financially and in terms of prestige. This is because a successful maiko will graduate into a successful geiko, drawing wealthy clients to the hanamachi, and thus benefiting the whole geisha community and the craft workers and others who depend on it.

After a prescribed series of apprentice stages, a maiko "changes her collar" at a formal ceremony marking her transition to geiko status. Geiko costume is more subdued than maiko, though still extremely elegant and rich. The *obi* is much shorter. In place of the maiko's

Above: An *ochaya* interior. Note the alcove (*tokonoma*) with hanging scroll. The one thing you will never see in an *ochaya* is a clock on the wall.

elaborately decorated hairstyle is a *katsura*, or wig. These are only worn for the first few years of geiko life, though. Footwear becomes more conservative, with *zori* sandals or lower clogs replacing the extravagant *okobo* platforms. Like maiko, geiko wear distinctive white makeup, though not so often, and not after the age of thirty. The overall look is less gorgeous, but more restrained and mature. (There is still a world of difference, however, between a geisha's kimono and an ordinary Japanese lady's formal wear.)

Geiko, while less gorgeously attired, are much more expert in dance, tea ceremony, and the other required arts. The more beautiful and talented geiko become *tachikata* (literally "standing person") geisha. At parties, they concentrate on dance. Less physically favored geiko sing or play the shamisen (a three-stringed Japanese instrument). These performers are known as *jikata* (literally "ground person") and normally work with *tachikata* geiko in informal working partnerships. All geiko, however, are expected both to be able to dance and to play shamisen, as these are basic, required skills. Most of all, geiko are expected to be masters in the art of entertainment and capable of livening up parties of even the most boring guests. Repartee, party games, and drinking games are all part of their stock in trade and as they mature in their craft, they quickly become expert in the art of timing, adjusting the flow to "keep the ball rolling."

As fully-fledged geisha, geiko use the social networks built up so painstakingly during their apprenticeships to develop a base of loyal customers who call on their services again and again. Once their debts to their parent geisha house are paid off, they can move out and be independent. Their earnings from party fees go directly to them, and they can keep tips from clients. Tipping is very rare in Japan and not done in restaurants or taxis. In the flower-and-willow world, however, it is almost mandatory and quite extravagant. A client will never tip below 10,000 Yen and can tip much more.

Party fees and tips provide a lucrative source of income for the geiko. However, maintaining a wardrobe and constantly adding new kimonos and accessories is an extremely expensive task. It is very difficult to stay in business as an independent geiko on party fees and tips alone. Traditionally, the way in which this problem was solved was to acquire a *danna* or patron. *Danna* is a slightly old-fashioned word meaning husband. However, in the flower-and-willow world, most *danna* were older, wealthy men and usually already married.

After formal negotiations through an *ochaya*, a *danna* entered into a contract with his chosen geiko, who thereby formally became his mistress. In return, the *danna* paid all the geiko's living, tuition, and wardrobe expenses. The

Geiko are expected to be masters in the art of entertainment.

Left: Japanese tea ceremony. The art form is closely linked to Buddhism.

question of commercial sex in the geisha world is the single most controversial problem in the whole discussion surrounding the flower-and-willow world.

Maiko are inseparable from Kyoto. Tokyo, however, is the home of one type of geisha almost unknown in Kyoto and now very rare on the ground indeed. This is the *taikomochi* (literally "drum carrier") or male geisha. The *taikomochi* tradition predates female geisha and it is similar in that their job is to liven up parties. The *taikomochi* makes a fascinating contrast to the stereotypical image of the Japanese male. Solemn and taciturn, the Japanese man carries more than a little of the samurai within himself and often needs copious alcoholic lubrication to relax in social situations. When he does, the path to drunken incoherence is often short and quick. The *taikomochi*, on the other hand, is a fountain of patter, both off-color and irreverent.

geisha continued to work as a performer and continued to earn performance fees.

The phenomenal expense involved restricted keeping a geisha to the very wealthy. Having a geisha mistress was a status symbol in Japan up until World War II. The practice officially passed away in 1959, when government-licensed prostitution in Japan was outlawed. In reality, however, prostitution remains very much a fact in Japan. The

Verbal pyrotechnics pile up on classical allusions and thoroughly obscene puns. This is fully in line with the light but educated *iki/tsu* aesthetic. Like hot-spring geisha, *taikomochi* developed a bad reputation as drunken flatterers or worse. They often sprang from the ranks of the geisha clients and entered the profession after bankrupting themselves in the flower-and-willow world. In the past, some were apparently not averse to fishing for clients by phoning them and inviting them to parties. This is a major faux pas in the flower-and-willow world, where geisha must wait for invitations. At their best, however, *taikomochi* are true geisha. They are officially registered as such, and they have a thorough grounding in the geisha arts and sensibility. There are only five or six of them left.

Preconceptions, Misconceptions, and Myths

To the world at large, the word geisha is first and foremost a symbol, far more than just a job. But what is it a symbol of? From the first stirrings of *Japonisme* in the nineteenth century, Western artists and writers have been drawn to the image of the geisha in a whole range of ways. The geisha as a pliable fantasy plaything for men: The geisha is seen as a tragic heroine or as an emissary of the Orient, replete with mysterious knowledge, cultural and sexual. The geisha is a postcard image of traditional Eastern woman, mingling Mount Fuji and the bullet train to form the image of twentieth-century Japan in the mind of the Western consumer.

The geisha as a vague composite of *Madame Butterfly* and Gilbert and Sullivan, prostitute and heroine, lives on in the English-speaking world, inspiring myriad pop reinterpretations. The most striking recent example was Madonna's approach to the geisha look at the 1999 Grammy Awards and her *Drowned* World Tour in 1999–2001. The centerpiece was a stunning red vinyl kimono with twenty-six meter

Above: *Japan—Autumn in Nikko*, a vintage poster for the travel agency Japan Travel Bureau. Kimono patterns are designed to match specific seasons. Tourist areas like Kyoto and Nikko strongly angle their marketing toward traditional aspects.

sleeves. The confection would have amused or horrified any real geisha who saw it.

The publication of Arthur Golden's novel *Memoirs of a Geisha* in 1997 was another landmark in the (re)creation of the modern image of the geisha. The book was a runaway bestseller, with over four million copies sold, and it was translated into thirty-three languages. The Western world experienced the biggest geisha boom in a century. Fashion writers rhapsodized over the kimono look and urged their readers to "geishaize." Stephen Spielberg was rumored to be interested in directing a movie of *Memoirs*. Yet at the same time, the reaction from the Japanese geisha world showed just how controversial the Western image of geisha could be.

Right: Maria Callas as Cio-Cio-San in *Madame Butterfly*. Puccini composed the opera shortly after witnessing a turn-of-the century geisha dancing.

Below: Arthur Golden, holding a *mahogi* (dance fan).

Iwasaki Mineko, a prominent ex-geisha who was Golden's main source on hanamachi life, was so incensed by his portrayal of geisha life and other comments he allegedly made in public that she launched a ten-million-dollar defamation suit against him and his publishers. The crux of the problem is the question of sex in the geisha world, and especially the question of *mizuage* or ceremonial deflowering.

Mizuage literally means "raising the waters," and in the past it referred to unloading a catch of fish or a ship's cargo. From there the word took to the stage, where it came to mean money earned in the entertainment business. The reason why it became deflowering in the hanamachi is that a geisha losing her virginity was not just a rite of passage: it was also a commercial transaction. Historically, a virgin geisha was a contradiction in terms. For an apprentice geisha to become fully qualified, she had to lose

her virginity to her patron (*danna*), if she had one. If not, the task fell to the highest bidder, who became her *mizuage danna*, or patron for the purpose of deflowering. Vast sums changed hands and there was nothing secretive about it. Like all payments in the hanamachi, it was officially recorded and published and a high price was a source of considerable pride for the girl's *okiya*. For the girl herself, *mizuage* was an ordeal, of course—but also a necessary rite of passage. Her hairstyle and clothing immediately changed, proclaiming her new, adult status to the hanamachi at large. She was normally aged between fifteen and seventeen.

The practice no longer exists. Since 1959, geisha's intimate lives are theirs alone to decide. Yet the Arthur Golden-Iwasaki Mineko debate has done nothing to enlighten Western opinion of what geisha are about. Geisha are still not seen primarily as artists, but as prostitutes. For Iwasaki, the breaking point was Golden's claim at a 1999 reading in Providence, Rhode Island, that she had told him that her *mizuage* price was about $850,000. She vehemently denied the statement, launched the suit, and also published her own memoir. Translated into English as *Geisha: A Life*, it insists on the geisha's dignity as a skilled performing artist and values the whole flower-and-willow world as a unique cultural treasure.

The many elements of the popular Western image of geisha all have a single common thread running through them: the idea of sex for sale. Japan has traditionally had—and still has—a flourishing red-light culture. Modern visitors to Japan are taken aback by the scale of

Above left: Iwasaki Mineko, the star Kyoto geisha of her generation.

Below left: Iwasaki Mineko in later life. Translated under the title *Sayuri, Memoirs of a Geisha* sold only 50,000 copies in Japan. Many members of the geisha community resented Golden's portrayal, and some blamed Iwasaki as she had been credited in the book as his principal informant.

Right: Prostitutes in the Shimabara district of Kyoto entertain a client. During the American Occupation, many described themselves as "geisha." This only added to the pre-existing confusions about the true role of geisha.

red-light districts which seem to exist in every town of any size. An enduring source of misunderstanding was the experience of American GIs in the occupation of Japan after World War II. Mass prostitution was a feature in those desperate days and many girls with no connection to the art passed themselves off as geisha to soldiers with no knowledge of that world apart from the word geisha itself. This pathetic reality is a far cry from the Madonna image of the geisha as an ultra-glamorized pop-goddess courtesan, yet the eroticism of the geisha is of course part of the mix in both cases. It remains

fair to say that the average perception of geisha in the English-speaking world is a hopeless tangle of wishful thinking, prurient curiosity, half-facts, and misconceptions.

Strangely enough, the picture is equally confused in Japan. Relatively few Japanese have ever seen a geisha in the flesh. Even fewer have the considerable financial resources needed to mix with geisha as patrons or regular customers. Fewer still have the background in traditional Japanese arts needed to fully appreciate and enjoy their private performances. And fewest of all break through the glass wall surrounding the flower-and-willow world. This barrier is summed up in the famous geisha phrase *ichigen-san o-kotowari*: No New Faces Accepted. For the flower-and-willow world is an exclusive club indeed and, like any gentlemen's club, can only be approached by means of recommendation from an established member.

For the average Japanese man or woman on the street, geisha belong to a separate reality, remote and inaccessible even for the minority who might wish to enter it. The typical Japanese man does indeed like to spend time with entertaining, glamorous women, and he has no qualms about paying for it. For this he goes not to the hanamachi, but to the hostess bar (more of which later). Hostesses can do without any background in the traditional arts that form the core of the geisha's professional identity. They tend to be totally modern, often dyed blonde—and sometimes naturally blonde— foreigners. Their company is relatively expensive, but it costs a pittance compared to a geisha's. They are above all undemanding and approachable, requiring none of the elaborate etiquette of the flower-and-willow world. In a way, hostess bars are the modern, popular equivalent.

Naturally, every Japanese has heard of geisha, and has some idea of what they look like. They feature in many novels and movies, especially historical ones. Tourists visiting Kyoto often look out for geisha and enjoy taking snaps of them if they happen to spot them on the street. Younger women take great pleasure in dressing up as apprentice geisha (for a

cost of 10,000–20,000 Yen) and strolling around the historic city. The problem is that they are often mistaken for the real thing and photographed accordingly. It is not so much that the Japanese public is losing its awareness of geisha. Rather, geisha have never been a feature of the ordinary person's life, and so the average tourist has no basis for comparison.

Novels and movies featuring geisha are usually set in the Tokugawa or Meiji periods, from 1600–1912. For hundreds of years, prostitution was an officially recognized, government-controlled fact of life. Even today, many Japanese marriages are arranged, more business contract than love match, and many Japanese men feel no shame in going to red-light districts (these are now unlicensed and mainly run by the *yakuza*). This was true even more so in former days. Monogamy was rarely the rule for men who could afford to indulge their tastes more broadly.

There may be no other country in which prostitution has played as important a cultural role as Japan. Among others, Edo had its famed Yoshiwara pleasure district and Kyoto had its Shimabara. This was the Floating World, and the top-class courtesans who lived in it were superstars, celebrated in songs, kabuki plays, and *ukiyo-e* prints. These courtesans, called *tayu* or *kottai* in Kyoto and *oiran* in Tokyo, set long-lasting standards for leisure culture. The urban culture of the Osaka merchant, the Kyoto craftsman, and the Edo shopkeeper revolved around the pleasure districts. Kabuki itself is a product of the Floating World, and in the past the actors were for sale. The geisha profession, too, is a

The flower-and-willow world is an exclusive club indeed.

Above: A prostitute in the historic Yoshiwara district of Tokyo. Post-war Japan was an exceptionally tough environment for many uprooted women.

country's social history. Geisha were no longer forced into the profession by parents who could not make ends meet, as was commonly the case until then. Entering the flower-and-willow world became purely a matter of choice. These days, young women join because of the glamorous image or a desire to practice the arts. The training is still very rigorous for modern young people though and the dropout rate is high. In the past, dropping out was not an option.

Even now, the geisha world remains associated with the hedonism of old. It is also true that present-day geishahood has a broad scope. Its apex is in the elite hanamachi of Kyoto, and there are prestigious geisha districts in Tokyo and some other major cities. Beyond that lies the world of the regional geisha, with more relaxed standards of training and lower levels of artistic achievement. Lowest on the prestige stakes are the *onsen* or hot-spring resort geisha, who are closely linked to prostitution—in popular opinion, at least.

It is also true that *danna* have not entirely disappeared from the scene. Anecdotal evidence suggests that perhaps one in five top-level geisha have patrons to support them in the old style. The practice is dying out, however. These days, more help comes from business sponsors who operate as a kind of fan club. In recent years, government help has also been forthcoming, in the shape of the Foundation for the Promotion of Traditional Artistic Accomplishments. It is popularly known in the hanamachi as the *Ookini Zaidan*, or "Thanks Very Much Foundation."

child of this era. The first geisha appeared in the mid-eighteenth century as dancers and shamisen players. Their special appeal was that they sold their artistic talents rather than their bodies, and they soon came to overshadow the courtesans. Unlike kabuki, however, the geisha world has never quite been able to throw off the old connections and become just Culture with a C. Both licensed prostitution and geisha parties flourished up until World War II.

The Anti-Prostitution Law of 1959 was much more than just an act of legislation. Its passage marked a fundamental break in the

Left: A hot-spring geisha attends to a guest during a meal. Geisha at popular spa resorts have a rather raunchy image, and are much looked down upon by the more elite members of the profession.

The popular Japanese image of geisha is based on historical fact and present realities. These, however, are thoroughly confused with each other; the idea of geisha, *tayu*, and *oiran* blends together, and all geisha are at some level lumped together with the popular stereotype of the hot-spring prostitute. Even where respected for their undoubted mastery of traditional dance, top-class geisha tend to be thought of as rich men's mistresses. This is close to the historical truth, but no longer the case. Geisha in the proper sense of the word have never been prostitutes; not being prostitutes was what originally defined them as geisha.

A World Apart

The confusion which most Japanese people feel about geisha is based on unfamiliarity. The flower-and-willow world is truly a world apart. Apart from major public festivals in Kyoto, and the occasional big company party in the provinces, very few people have the chance to experience it. The number of men who regularly attend *ozashiki* parties is very small indeed. Like yacht racing or polo, this is a pastime for the few.

This unfamiliarity with the geisha world heightens Japanese sensitivities when talking about it to foreigners. On the whole, the Japanese are very self-conscious about what the outside world thinks of them. They are also very touchy about negative stereotyping. The whole geisha question is one that many people prefer not to discuss. The phrase *Fujiyama Geisha* is used in Japan as a despairing catch-phrase summarizing Western obsessions and preconceptions about the country. The visiting Westerner often incorrectly calls *Fuji-san* "*Fujiyama*." In the same way, traditional culture is simplistically reduced to the fantasy dancer/call-girl figure of the geisha. Japanese people's touchiness on this point is heightened by insecurity, because very few Japanese themselves are really sure about what geisha do.

Japan boasts many artistic and sporting worlds that resemble the flower-and-willow world. Kabuki drama and sumo, for example, are equally traditional, rigidly hierarchical, and daunting to enter. Like geisha craft, both of them function as time machines in a sense. Kabuki, for example, has preserved costumes props and language unchanged for centuries, and functions as a wonderful resource for historians. More importantly, these living time machines preserve not just the art form or sport itself, but equally the lifestyle of bygone ages, with their elaborate courtesies and fearsome disciplines. Indeed, all Japanese arts, from calligraphy to tea ceremony to judo are strictly controlled by licensed *sensei* (teachers), yet these three pastimes have mass appeal in modern society, and are in no danger of dying out.

Right: Kabuki theater. The all-male kabuki world is closely connected to its female counterpart, the flower-and-willow world. Kabuki provides both customers and dance styles.

Left: A traditional Japanese environment—tatami matting, sliding paper doors, and an exterior garden.

The flower-and-willow world, however, may be in serious trouble. The number of geisha is plummeting. Kabuki and sumo are performance arts, but geisha performance is performance art of a very special kind. The intimate teahouse party requires a highly-educated audience that participates in making the gathering work. It cannot work as a museum piece. Yet as Japanese society changes, the kind of client that geisha need is becoming rarer and rarer. The whole flower-and-willow world is in danger of becoming an island from another age, cut off by the waters of change.

Geisha life differs from the mainstream in many other ways, and sometimes has a *Through the Looking Glass* quality to it as viewed from standard Japan. This is a world where women have the command and marriage does not exist. All geisha retire if and when they marry, and there is none of the traditional stigma attached in Japan to spinsterhood. Nor are any eyebrows raised at single motherhood, which even today is extremely rare in mainstream society and still rather disapproved of. When a child is born, girls are preferred. Girls are potential geisha, whereas boys have few to zero options in the hanamachi. The traditional Confucian outlook that valued boys over girls and obsessed on continuing the family name is thankfully almost dead in modern Japan. In the geisha world, it never stood a chance.

In terms of language, also, the flower-and-willow world stands apart. Maiko often have trouble using the proper dialect, even if they come from Kyoto originally. The Japanese of the Kyoto hanamachi is a dialect unto itself. Resembling the Western dialects of the Kansai region, it is softer, more feminine, and contains many special terms unknown to outsiders. *Arigato* (thank you) is *ooki ni*; *desu* (to be) is *dosu*. Even the word for "yes" is different; *hai* becomes *hei*. "Grease bugs" infest the *ochaya* kitchens—these are customers who hang around hoping to speak more with geisha without being willing to pay. Drunken or horrible guests are "electricity poles in thunder" for the trouble and anxiety they cause the unfortunate maiko and geiko who have to entertain them. [2]

Above: Senior and junior. In formally posed East Asian photographs, the senior partner occupies the centre of the picture— as in this postcard of geisha and rickshaw driver.

A World In Common

Although it is a different planet in many ways, the flower-and-willow world did not, obviously, fall from the sky. It was born out of Japanese society and must continue to find its way there. Studies of geisha usually concentrate only on their differences from the mainstream. Yet a great deal about them can be understood by looking at them as normal Japanese people, living extraordinary lives. Here some aspects of geisha life are discussed which are almost invisible to Japanese commentators, because they form basic parts of the life of every member of the society.

Senior-Junior relationships: The elder brother-younger brother bond is one of the five basic human relationships in Confucianism, and it holds great importance in one form or another for all East Asians. In Japan, it is more a question of seniority than age. If B joins a group one day after A, B is *kohai* (junior) and A is *senpai* (senior) as long as their association lasts— and it may well last for life. Juniors must use the correct language, bows, and greetings when talking with seniors. This is true in the most elegant geisha teahouse, true in the grayest bureaucrat's office, and equally true in the toughest biker gang. To a Westerner it may sound robotic and harsh, but the relationship can be—and very often is—a warm one. Seniors are expected to look out for juniors and guide their progress. In return, juniors should respect the advice given them, do chores, run errands, and so forth. There is always the danger that seniors may bully their juniors, or that juniors may disregard their seniors and trouble often results. But many Japanese friendships are based on this relationship, and they can be very close even while observing the niceties.

In the Kyoto hanamachi, maiko take geiko as Older Sisters in a ceremony that closely resembles a wedding, with three formal toasts of sake. These mentors sometimes come from different *okiya*, so the relationship can be distinct from the family hierarchy of the geisha house. Since there is no man in the house, the *okiya* family structure is quite bizarre in Japanese terms (single-parent families, as mentioned earlier, are still a tiny minority). However, the Mother or Grandmother is still very much the traditional authority figure. Her rule can be of iron, as befits a family with a lifestyle straight from the past. The most senior geiko, however, gets special privileges, often in the form of extra living space. Her earnings may be supporting the whole house.

The Japanese language divides the world into two—inside and outside, *uchi* and *soto*. *Uchi* is inside the family, inside the company, inside the *okiya*. And *soto* is the world outside. The language also divides the world into upper and lower honorific positions. When seniors do something, they "condescend to do" it (*shite kureru*); when juniors do something, they "offer up" the action (*shite ageru*). Inside the *uchi* (the family, school, and so on) there are seniors and juniors. However, in relations with the outside world, the *soto*, one must present the whole *uchi* as lower in honorific position. Thus, "The milk-

man condescended to deliver milk to our (miserable) home" would not sound strange in Japanese—if only milkmen existed.

What this means in practice in the hanamachi is that formal visits to *ochaya* and other *okiya*, and formal greetings on the street, are of the highest importance. A great deal of a maiko's work involves tripping around the hanamachi in her *okobo* platform clogs, giving the correct, respectful greetings to the people she will need to get to know to succeed as a geiko.

A beautiful example of honorific practice is the *taikomochi*'s (male geisha's) use of his fan. On entering a party room, he makes a formal bow on his knees and places the fan on the floor before him, between himself and the guests. This act symbolically splits the level tatami mat surface in two, honorifically higher and lower. The *taikomochi*'s place is of course

Below: A young maiko stands with an older woman, probably a former geisha who now trains young women in the traditional arts.

Right: A traditional Kyoto streetscape.

lower and the guests' higher. Maiko and geiko use their fans in a similar way with their dance teachers.

Using honorific language is tricky, even for native speakers. Older people regularly lament the decline in younger peoples' skills. For example, a boss will always be referred to by an employee as President Tanaka. On the phone to a client, however, he must be referred to as Tanaka, with no honorific phrases. Younger Japanese often slip up; in the flower-and-willow world, no such mistakes are permissible. To an older generation of Japanese, this carefulness with language is far from being petty or narrow-minded. It is a question of giving each person their due, of being able to behave like a fully adult member of society. The hanamachi are bastions of correct honorific Japanese, and the Kyoto hanamachi are perhaps the only

arena left where this language is used in a community, on the street.

Cooperation is vital for hierarchical relationships to work. Japanese society waxes lyrical on the idea of social harmony, from kindergarten to retirement party. "All together" and "pooling our power" are everyday phrases in Japan, where group effort is so important and valued. This commitment to cooperation whatever the cost to one's self is what holds the *okiya* together despite the tensions of living in a rigidly stratified environment.

Endurance: This rigid lifestyle calls for a great deal of endurance, another key idea in Japanese culture. The phrases *gambare* (push yourself) and *gaman suru* (stick it out) crop up many times every day in people's conversations. Pushing oneself and sticking it out are forms of morality in Japanese life, and the object of all this striving is of no importance whatsoever. College students might spend a sleepless week designing a fantastically complex domino display; office workers will be called upon to work until ten or eleven at night. It is the quality of the commitment rather than the end result that counts. Endurance is a quality much called for in the hanamachi and maiko in particular are incredibly busy people. Their rounds of classes, formal visits, and evening parties may leave them with only two or three hours sleep a night. The answer is to *gambare*. Competitive spite and fierce teachers are facts of hanamachi life. What to do? *Gaman suru.*

Perfectionism and imitation: In all walks of Japanese life, it is understood that there is one, and only one, perfect way to do anything. The Western visitor to Japan may get a rather eerie feeling as every waitress in every café places every cup of coffee or tea on the table in exactly the same fashion. It is a set form. In the arts, including the martial arts, it is called a *kata*. The most celebrated example in the flower-and-willow world is the way in which geisha kneel to slide a door open and closed when they enter a room. Every aspect of their posture is set, from the angle at which the arm is held to the position of the knees on the floor. Proper performance of the *kata* is not at all robotic. It is an expression of respect for the guest, and for one's own role as a host, all the more sincere for being punctiliously enacted. In the Japanese arts, where the body leads, the heart follows, and not vice versa.

The origins of this attitude lie in Zen Buddhism, which put down deep roots in

samurai culture. Tea ceremony, calligraphy, and Japanese archery are all cases in point. The archer will bow, enter the room, and kneel to put on his glove exactly the same way each time, and every other action is equally prescribed. Constant, minutely controlled repetition of the same task allows the practitioner to finally break through the barrier of the ego, and to discard it—if only for an instant. Something of this approach remains even in the way students practice baseball or waitresses serve coffee.

Matriarchy: A typical Japanese "salaryman" receives his pay packet, and that evening presents it to his wife. Or these days, it is more often sent to their joint bank account. In either case, control of the money will immediately devolve to the woman of the house. She doles out an appropriate amount of pocket money to the husband. He neither contests nor complains. Rather, if unsatisfied, he tries to earn money on the side. This money is called

Below: A Tokyo geisha. All members of the flower-and-willow world are expected to be impeccably turned out at all times.

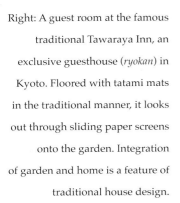
Right: A guest room at the famous traditional Tawaraya Inn, an exclusive guesthouse (*ryokan*) in Kyoto. Floored with tatami mats in the traditional manner, it looks out through sliding paper screens onto the garden. Integration of garden and home is a feature of traditional house design.

hesokuri, or "belly button stash." Control of the household rests with women in Japan, and many decisions are taken in token consultation with the husband. In another example of *uchi* (inside) and *soto* (outside), the roles are divided. The husband sees to *soto*; the wife takes care of *uchi*. As the saying goes, *shujin wa soto de, rusu ga yoi*: the husband belongs outside, and should be out of the house (earning money).

In the public world, the *soto*, men rule: *danson johi* (respect the man, despise the woman). This saying is no longer a true picture of how people act. Yet something of the etiquette remains, and opportunities for women remain much more limited than in the West. *Danna* is an old word for husband; yet even today, the standard word for husband in Japanese is *go-shujin*—honorable master. Within the household, however, matriarchy is often the norm. The flower-and-willow world, devoid of men in power, is a special case. Yet the domestic rule of Mother or Grandmother is not at all a foreign concept in Japan.

The seasons: Foreign visitors to Japan are often taken aback when asked: "Do you have four seasons in your country?" The seasons are part of the ideology of Japanese-ness, and the questioner will be vaguely surprised, or reassured, to be told that yes, we too have spring, summer, fall, and winter. Japanese culture treasures the seasons and marks their passage with a host of annual events and changes in cuisine. Even modern consumer culture shows no signs of changing the trend. TV commercials inveigle consumers with this season's snack foods, beer flavors, and car colors.

The seasons are important to the hanamachi in two ways. Firstly, the Kyoto hanamachi and others revolve through a set series of annual events: formal visits to the dance master in January, Gion Festival in July, and so on. Secondly, the custom of marking the passage of the seasons is deeply embedded in all traditional Japanese arts. Haiku poems composed in spring contain different set seasonal words from those composed in, say, early summer. Fall kimonos will have a range of colors, patterns, and motifs distinguishable at a glance from winter ones. Maiko and geiko invest in the seasons. Apart from appropriate kimonos, fans, parasols, and so on, maiko change their elaborate hair ornaments every month. The expense may be exceptional, but the attention paid to seasonal change is in line with society at large.

Cleanliness: In Japan's Shinto religion, cleanliness is not next to godliness. The simple reason is that there is no discernable difference between the two. Shinto has nothing to say about good and evil. Rather, it offers ways to preserve ritual cleanliness and exorcize ritual defilement. Geisha, like all Japanese, celebrate the Setsubun festival in February, driving evil spirits out (to *soto*, that is) by scattering dried beans around the house. Like sumo wrestlers, they use salt to keep bad luck away, and get lightly doused with it when they return from funerals. Cleaning the most unclean place, the toilet, has special meaning for traditionally minded people. Thus Iwasaki Mineko, later to become the star of Gion:

Below: A troupe of women dancers wear traditional kimonos at a cherry blossom festival in Kyoto.

Wearing brightly colored kimonos, geisha perform a dance as part of Kyoto's Cherry Dances. This premier event has been a staple of the Kyoto calendar since the 1870s.

Right: A hostess bar in Tokyo. It is quite acceptable for staff members to drink on the job in most Japanese bars. The customer is most likely a regular who drops in to unwind once or twice a week.

Besides taking lessons, I also cleaned the toilets every morning…Cleaning is considered a vital part of the training process in all traditional Japanese disciplines and is a required practice for any novice. It is accorded spiritual significance. Purifying an unclean place is believed to purify the mind. [3]

Work and Play in Modern Japan

The Japanese clearly divide the world into senior and junior, inside and outside, higher and lower. Another clear and important division in Japanese life is between work and play. The Japanese are well known in the West for their workaholic tendencies. Stories of unfortunate salarymen dying of *karoshi*—literally being worked to death—regularly appear in English. Less famous, however, is their prodigious ability for seizing life's pleasures. If any nation plays as hard as it works, it is Japan.

As Ruth Benedict put it in *The Chrysanthemum and the Sword*, her classic anthropological study of Japan:

The Japanese do not condemn self-gratification. They are not Puritans. They consider physical pleasures good and worthy of cultivation. They are sought and valued. Nevertheless, they have to be kept in their place. They must not intrude upon the serious affairs of life. [4]

This idea of the innate goodness of physical pleasure does not produce a nation of debauchees with Mr Hyde faces behind Doctor Jekyll masks. Most of the pleasures Benedict discusses are entirely innocent, like the evening bath or April cherry-blossom viewing. Nevertheless, Japan remains quite different from the West in having never gone through a truly puritanical historical phase. Nor is this the only difference in the schema of things. Pleasures on their own are not enough. They have to be learned, just as much as politeness. Otherwise they do not fit in with one's (serious) life as a whole. This sensibility is by now very traditional, but still strong in the flower-and-willow world:

> Americans do not believe that pleasures have to be learned…[The Japanese] cultivate the pleasures of the flesh like fine arts, and then, when they are fully savored, they sacrifice them to duty. [5]

In modern Japan, this picture represents only the cultured elite. The flower-and-willow world is out of the reach of all but the few. The relentless busyness of the modern Japanese lifestyle allows very little free time for the average person. Even so, traditional aesthetic pleasures like tea ceremony, flower arranging, and haiku poetry still command mass appeal, as do martial arts and sports.

But above all, the word *asobi* (play) conjures up an image of Japanese nightlife in all its occasionally sordid variety. Relatively little entertaining is done at home, partly because housing is often cramped. But more fundamentally, the world of play is *soto* (outside). One goes out for *asobi*. Husbands and wives usually socialize separately. It would be almost unheard of for spouses and girlfriends or boyfriends to be invited to company functions, for example.

Left: A typical day scene in the Gion district of Kyoto.

Right: Many hostesses work
in traditional clothing.

Once out on the town, not all the available pleasures are innocent, either for men or for women. At the bottom of the barrel, every size-able Japanese town has its quota of brothels or massage parlors. These are referred to as "soap-lands" or more recently *herusu* (health saunas). They used to be known as *torko*, or Turkish baths, until repeated protests from the offended country forced a change in name. Strip clubs are also common, catering to women also. This is the world of *mizu shobai* (the Water Trade), in other words the sex trade.

The vast middle ground is occupied by the hostess bar, or more rarely, the host bar for ladies. This is a kind of recreation with no exact equivalent in the West. A hostess bar is a fairly small establishment, with a *mama-san* and per-haps five or six young(ish) women staff. They may wear kimonos or Versace, but they will be elegant in the house style. This can be anything from sub-geisha to bleach blonde and micro-minis. The customers are usually regulars, often with their own bottle of whisky stored behind the counter. A regular may drop in once or twice a week, to be greeted by name, agreeably fussed over and chatted to. This massage for the ego which is often much-needed by the harassed salaryman and is essentially what the customer pays for.

Westerners often presume that hostess bars are brothels of some kind. This is a misunder-standing, but not a complete one. Most men visit hostess bars not for sex as such, but for the promise of sex, for the simple *frisson* of being familiar with and pampered by an elegant younger woman. For most customers, that is quite enough. If a man wants more, there is no shortage of other places for him to take his business. Nevertheless, there is a strong connection in the average Japanese person's mind between hostess bars and the Water Trade. It's very common for customers and hostesses to become lovers. It's also very common for their love to have a flourishing commercial aspect. The line between what is and isn't prostitution can get very blurred. Even if money isn't involved, any hostess worth her salt will be showered with gifts from customers, whether they are lovers or not. Some can be very extravagant (sports cars and shopping sprees are not unknown).

Any geisha worth her salt will vehemently deny that there is any connection between the world of the hostess bar and the flower-and-willow world—and with good reason. The hostess has none of the grounding in the arts that are a geisha's stock-in-trade. The hostess may be a mini-skirted eighteen-year-old, with a knowledge of Japanese tradition stretching back as far as Pokemon. Top-level geisha earn fortunes that make the Water Trade an irrelevance anyway. For them, the raunchier hot-spring geisha, who sometimes resemble hostesses, are not the real thing.

The real connection between the hostess and the geisha is almost invisible to Japanese eyes. In both cases, the customer is paying for fun and companionship, without necessarily

expecting any sexual favors. The atmosphere tends to have a playfully erotic edge, skillfully handled with a knowing, often teasing, and not unkind air. From there, the roads part company. The trained geisha, or the maiko or *hangyoku*, is working with a range of skills in a different stratosphere from the hostess, and at best, her customers have been educated to appreciate what she's doing. She is the caviar of Japanese entertainment. As Oscar Wilde wrote fondly of the cigarette, the geisha offers something quite different: "the perfect type of a perfect pleasure. It is exquisite, and leaves one unsatisfied. What more could one want?" Had he been born Japanese, Wilde would surely have been that rarest of creatures, the man of *tsu*.

Above: Businessmen relaxing after a hard day at the office. This kind of bonding is part of their job. Many get home so late from work that their children only meet them at breakfast.

CHAPTER 1

geisha quarters: the hanamachi

Geisha life takes place in a kind of labyrinth.

Right: Geisha at a festival in Shimoda, near Tokyo. Shimoda was the hometown of the tragic geisha heroine Okichi.

Far right: A miniature of hanamachi life: an elder geisha enjoys a little people watching, while a younger partner adjusts her summer kimono.

It is a city made only of exceptions, exclusions, incongruities, contradictions.

Italo Calvino, *Invisible Cities*

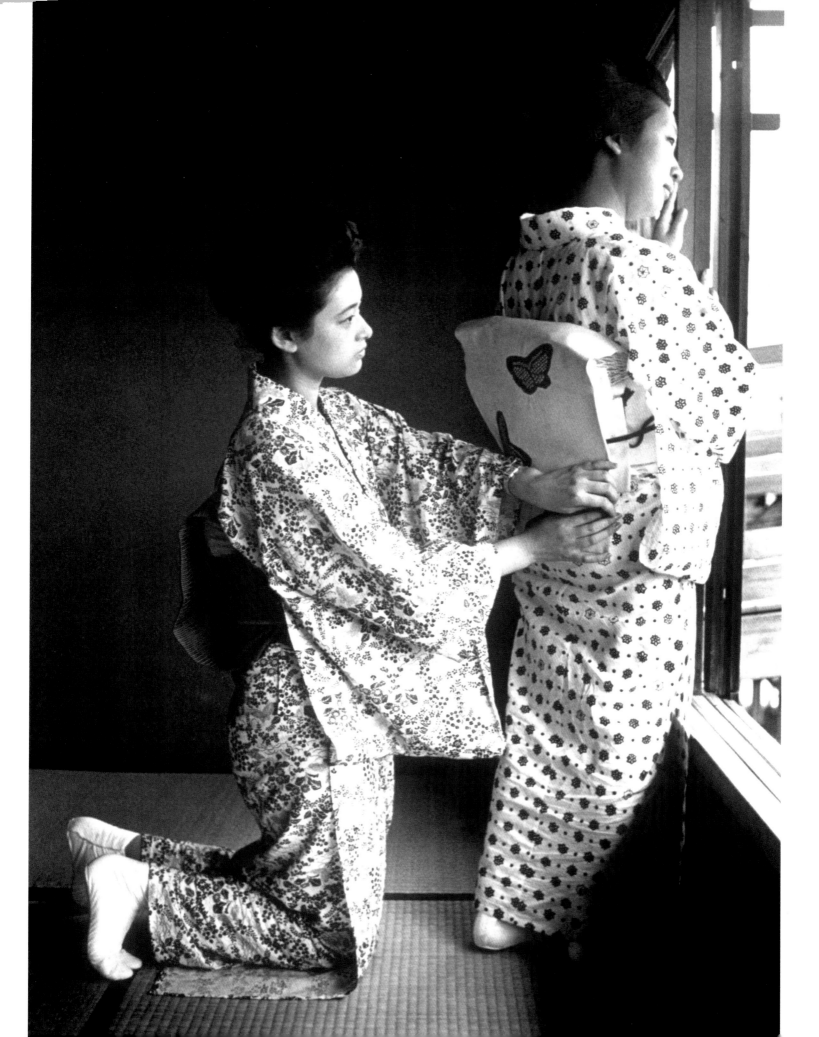

Flower Towns: The Hanamachi

Geisha life, and Kyoto geisha life especially, takes place in a kind of labyrinth: the hanamachi or geisha quarters. Hanamachi literally means "flower town." Flowers have always had an erotic image, not just in Japan but in East Asia as a whole. In Chinese literature, for example, visiting the pleasure quarters was called "viewing the flowers." In modern Japan, city-center florists stay open late into the night, doing a brisk trade in bouquets. The customers are "salarymen" and the floral tributes are destined for the hostess bar. The flower-and-willow world is a good deal more tasteful in its approach. But the object of the exercise is still the creation of a fantasy world. In the flower towns, every guest can fancy himself a romantic prince of the fabulously elegant, decadent Heian Era. The teahouse provides the setting and the geisha is the catalyst. The fantasy may never be satisfied but it is all the more exquisite for that.

Right: Japanese tourists to Kyoto regularly enjoy dressing up and trying out the maiko look.

Ministry of Beauty: The Bureaucracy of the Hanamachi

However romantic the name, the reality of the flower town is of necessity more down-to-earth. In legal terms, a hanamachi is an urban district containing a group of licensed geisha-related institutions. It has its own local administration, which sees to booking, registration, finance, and event management. Each hanamachi is autonomous. They have no local government powers as such; their remit covers geisha affairs only. They wield a great deal of economic power in their urban districts though. In recent years, they often receive government support through the *Ookini Zaidan* or local equivalent organizations.

The scale of the Kyoto hanamachi, with 190 *ochaya* (teahouses) altogether ° make them important players, though the numbers are in decline. Their real economic clout becomes apparent when one considers the vast range of support professions that depend in part or entirely on the flower-and-willow world. Kimono textile painters, kimono fabric dealers and salespeople, specialist wigmakers, hair ornament makers, makeup producers, and caterers are highly dependent on geisha custom. The kimono crafts are especially so because of the sheer volume of top-of-the-range garments they sell into the hanamachi; there are really no other takers for a kimono at seven million yen. The collapse of the hanamachi would lead to an equal, disastrous collapse in high-level kimono production expertise; the custom would simply vanish.

Left: Kako Moriguchi is a National Living Treasure and considered one of Japan's greatest living kimono artists. Moriguchi works in the traditional Kyo-yuzen dyeing method. Here he is painting a design on a silk kimono.

There are more specialized trades too, like *ochaya* staff (including sake warmers and *nakai*, who serve the food and drinks), geisha dressers (*otokosu*), and painters of *mokuroku* posters. These are colorful affairs, with beautiful calligraphy, which are posted to celebrate a maiko's debut. These professions are completely dependent on the flower-and-willow world. Ominously, they are in serious decline. Geisha dressers and specialist poster painters are almost extinct. There are five or six dressers still active in Kyoto, and only one *mokuroku* painter. Ironically, these are two of the very few professions for men in the hanamachi, if one discounts the equally rare *taikomochi* (male geisha).

With its host of shrines, temples, and traditional arts institutions, Kyoto also employs

Right: A geisha in Kyoto buying some gum at a small shop at the train station.

more than its share of dance and music teachers, tea ceremony and flower arrangement
teachers, calligraphers, gardeners, florists, and
makers of traditional accessories like fans and
parasols. These have customers outside the
flower-and-willow world, but do considerable
amounts of their business within it. The hanamachi are prime consumers of top-line traditional luxury goods and services, and their
decline could seriously damage a whole swathe
of linked crafts and traditions.

Apart from the *ochaya* and *okiya*, a full-scale
hanamachi contains schools for dance and
shamisen, a theater for geisha performances,
and, like every Japanese district, a number of
Shinto shrines and Buddhist temples. The
flower-and-willow world is relatively devout

by Japanese standards; also, the shrines often
play a part in the organization of the hanamachi. The most powerful artistic institution in
the hanamachi is the dance school. Apprentices
who cannot master the basics do not become
qualified geisha. The Inoue School of dance
in particular is a power in the land, and the
official school of Gion Kobu, Kyoto's most
prestigious hanamachi.

In days gone by, discipline in the training
institutions was very tough. It was not
unknown for teachers to slap students who
were not performing well—or even to slap students who were performing well to make them
perform better. A more psychological and
equally effective approach is the dread command *otome*! (You will kindly *desist*!) barked at

The main kimono is patterned according to the season; patterns for maiko are relatively elaborate. The *obi* (sash) is worn over the *obi-age*, which helps keep it in position. The narrow braid worn over the obi is called the *obi-jime*. It is decorated with a clasp called the *pocchiri*. The footwear is *okobo* platform clogs. The red thongs indicate that the maiko is relatively new to the profession.

The main undergarment is the
nagajuban, a full-length under-
kimono that follows the same line
as the garment over it. A collar or
eri is stitched on. Maiko *nagajuban*
are typically red with a white floral
print design.

The main undergarment is the nagajuban, a full-length under-kimono that follows the same line as the garment over it. A collar or eri is stitched on. Maiko nagajuban are typically red with a white floral print design.

The *hadajuban* resembles a buttonless blouse. It is worn right side folded over left, as with all traditional Japanese clothes. The slip covering the legs is popularly known as a *susoyoke*.

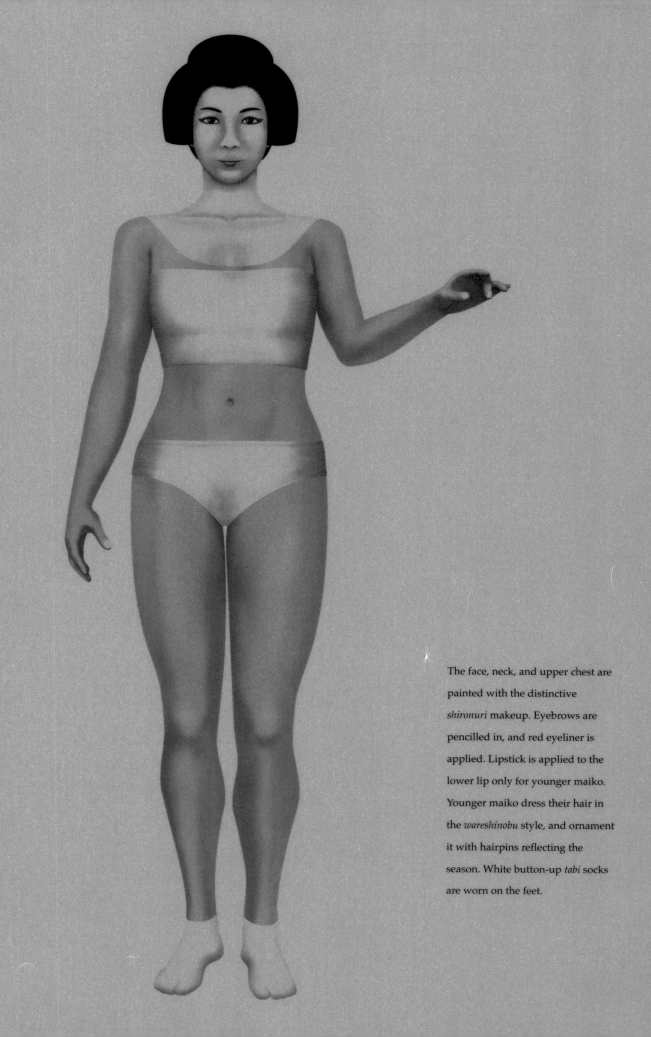

The face, neck, and upper chest are painted with the distinctive *shironuri* makeup. Eyebrows are pencilled in, and red eyeliner is applied. Lipstick is applied to the lower lip only for younger maiko. Younger maiko dress their hair in the *wareshinobu* style, and ornament it with hairpins reflecting the season. White button-up *tabi* socks are worn on the feet.

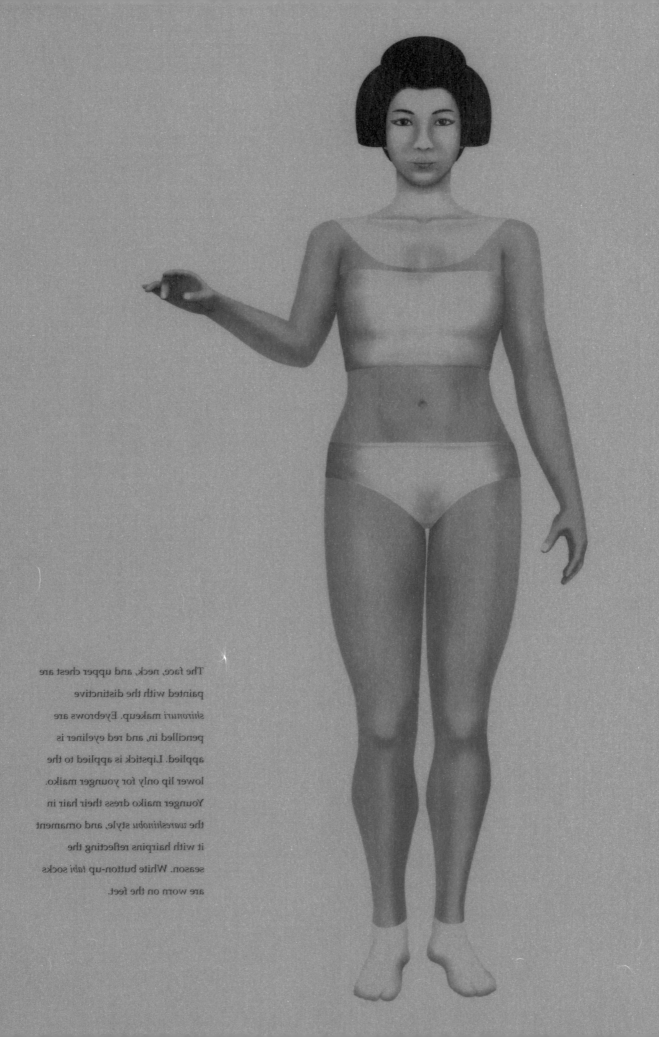

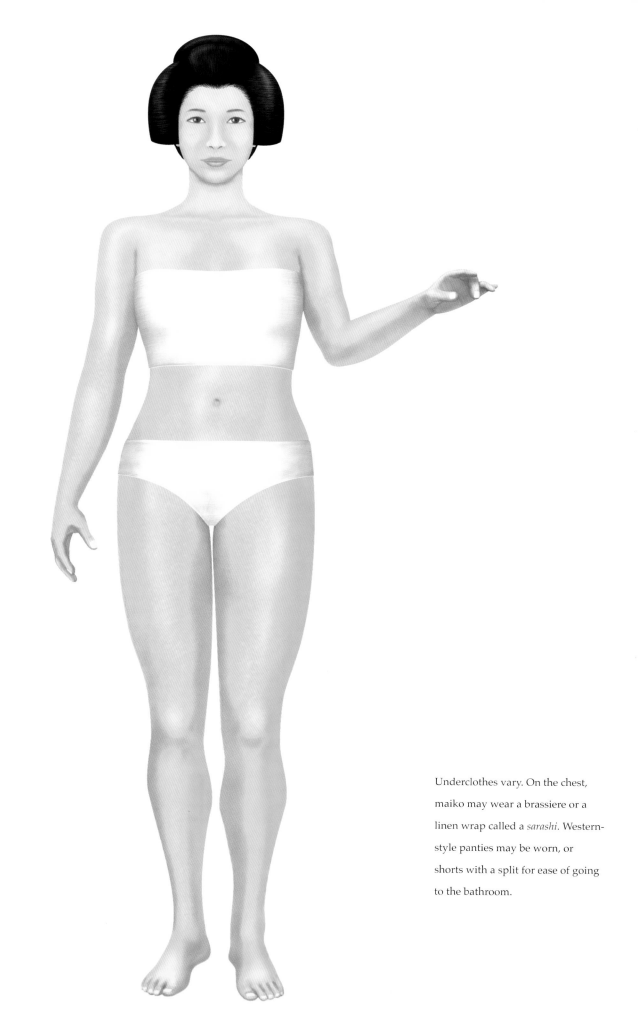

Underclothes vary. On the chest, maiko may wear a brassiere or a linen wrap called a *sarashi*. Western-style panties may be worn, or shorts with a split for ease of going to the bathroom.

the under-performing maiko. Class stops on the spot. The offender's *okiya* Mother is summoned and the unfortunate girl is hauled off for an indefinite (but usually short) suspension. In former times, it was all accompanied by much wailing and gnashing of teeth. Not so these days; a maiko upset by a tongue-lashing may well opt to go home to her birth family. Maiko, no longer legally indentured servants, are now far too rare a treasure to be lost so carelessly.

Below: A maiko in a Gion street.

Hanamachi finances and certification come under the supervision of a *kemban*. There are many different translations of this term—geisha registry office, geisha call-office, or exchange, and so on. The Chinese characters literally mean "inspection of order." Essentially, the *kemban* functions as the auditor for the hanamachi as a whole. It tallies how much each geisha or trainee earns and it posts the results publicly. These matter enormously to the geisha in terms of their professional pride. In its own way, the flower-and-willow world is as brutal as sumo; there is no hiding from the results. The *kemban*'s other role is registration of geisha and maiko. Rather like France or Italy, Japan is a highly bureaucratic country. The simplest forms and certificates are invariably embossed with multiple elaborate seals in red, and the papers matter.

The *kemban*'s ability to strike a professional off the register is power indeed. With Japan's emphasis on harmony, compromise, and negotiated settlements, this power is rarely used. Nevertheless, the *taikomochi* Yugentei Tamasuke [7] relates the tale of an apprentice of his who got himself embroiled in a love affair with a geisha. This involves two hanamachi faux pas. Firstly, the apprentice *taikomochi* could not concentrate on amusing the guests at parties where his lover was performing; he always ended up deeply engrossed in conversation with the beauteous geisha instead. Secondly, the young man's "secret" assignations (there are no secrets in the hanamachi) were a form of theft from her geisha house. Every moment of a geisha's time with a man must be paid for—under any circumstances. The *kemban* got word of the story and warned Tamasuke, who in turn passed the heat on to his apprentice but to no avail. Eventually, the *kemban* struck off the apprentice. The ban did not just extend to Tokyo. He was barred from employment in any of the hanamachi in Japan.

The *kemban* is not, however, the governing body of the hanamachi. In the last resort, the hanamachi is run by a consortium of the local Association of Teahouse Owners and the Geiko Association (or equivalent organization outside Kyoto). Gion Kobu is managed as a consortium of the above two groups along with the Kabukai, an educational foundation which controls the hanamachi's famed geisha school, the Yasaka Nyokoba Academy.

In most sizeable hanamachi, the various key institutions occupy buildings within a stone's throw of each other. In many cases, they share a large building called the *kaburenjo* (place for music and dance rehearsal). It houses the dance school, theater, *kemban*, and the Association of Teahouse Owners and Geisha Association.

The hanamachi, then, is an intricate labyrinth of institutions, like a medieval patchwork of fiefs and kingdoms. The apprentice geisha must learn to navigate each and every one. This complexity is only natural in an institution several centuries old, with even deeper roots stretching back into Japan's feudal past. This elaborate machinery is not kept in public view. Nor is it what people come to see in any case.

The Kyoto Hanamachi

All major Japanese cities have their hanamachi. But it is in Kyoto that the flower towns keep their original texture and shape, though the years are gradually shrinking them into bonsai versions of their former selves. The five Kyoto hanamachi are Gion Kobu (Upper Gion), Gion Higashi (East Gion), Ponto-cho, Miyagawa-cho, and Kami Shichiken. One more, Shimabara, no longer functions as a working geisha district, though it preserves the remains of an even older tradition—the *tayu* courtesan.

Gion Kobu and Gion Higashi

Kyoto was founded in 792 and modeled on the Chinese capital of the time, Xian. Like its continental model, it was laid out in a grid pattern, making it unusually easy to navigate for a Japanese city. At the north end of the grid lies the old Imperial Palace. At the south end is the much unloved Kyoto Station, a massive, brutally futuristic monstrosity. The eastern side of the

Left: Inside a geisha amusement restaurant in the Gion quarter of Kyoto.

grid is defined by the Kamo River. About halfway between the Palace and Kyoto Station runs Shijo-dori (Fourth Street), from east to west. Follow Shijo-dori over the Kamo River and you enter Gion, Kyoto's most famous historic district. The venerable Minamiza kabuki theater stands immediately past the Kamo bridge. From there Shijo-dori runs straight through Gion Kobu about 500 meters to Yasaka Shrine, where it finishes. Tucked off to the left of Shijo-dori lies Gion Higashi. Gion is pronounced with a hard g, and rhymes with neon; the shi in Higashi reads like English "she."

Hanamachi started as service areas for travelers. The beginnings of Japanese tourism lie in the mid-sixteenth century when Kyoto was the nation's biggest city and Tokyo-to-be was just a village of a thousand peasants among the swamps of the Kanto plain. Just as in medieval Europe, pilgrimage was the chief excuse for travel. Gion was close to a main pilgrim artery

terminating nearby. Visitors were also drawn to the Yasaka Shrine, dedicated to the Shinto gods Susano-o-no-mikoto, Kushi-inada-hime-no-mikoto, and Yahashirami-ko-no-kami. As the number of visitors increased, some very simple restaurants opened on Shijo-dori leading up to the shrine. These were called *mizujaya* (water and teahouses) and are the ancestors of today's *ochaya*. They were open to any member of the public, who ate the simple fare provided sitting on raised tatami pallets. By the time they were formally licensed around 1665, they had become considerably more sophisticated. Alcohol was served by girls who also danced in kabuki-style and played shamisen. Their red aprons, tied at the front, hinted at other services on offer. In fact, the teahouses were starting to become an informal rival to the officially licensed Shimabara pleasure district on the other side of the city. Teahouse patrons were now served not in open view of the public, but

Right: Maiko attending a blessing of bamboo leaves at a Shinto shrine. Most Japanese people observe both Buddhism and Shinto simultaneously.

in rooms deeper inside the premises. The customers' tastes had expanded far beyond mere prayer. Apart from the teahouses (and perhaps their maids) they also enjoyed cherry blossom and fall leaf viewing, along with the stocks and severed heads on display at the nearby Shijogawara, Kyoto's premier place of execution. The teahouses no longer had working kitchens; the cooking was handed over to outside caterers. By the time the first female geisha appeared in Edo, all the elements of the hanamachi system were in place and ready to

expand. Geisha were formally licensed to perform in Kyoto in 1813. The number of geiko and maiko soon reached three thousand in Gion alone.

Gion impresses itself on the Japanese psyche in a number of ways. Firstly the physical beauty of its traditional architecture is a treasure. Japan is a land of cities leveled time and again by earthquake and bombing. Rebuilt again and again, they now really resemble the anonymous block cities of Japanese video games. Most of this has passed Gion by, and it

Above: A kabuki *onnagata* (a man playing the role of a woman) is helped with his wig. Kabuki is the most popular form of traditional Japanese theater and has influenced many geisha dance styles.

仕入帳　大福帳

Above: Maiko in traditional costume perform the Ponto-cho Odori dance. The performances feature both male and female characters, but all roles are played by women. The performer on the left wears the distinctive *mae-ware* wig employed by geisha when playing male characters.

shares Venice's quandary of being beautiful and swamped with tourists. The concentration of nearby temples still draws people, just as it did over 400 years ago. Kabuki is inseparable from the Minamiza. Above all, Gion appears in TV dramas. Japanese TV drama is a formulaic, anemic beast and every episode set in Kyoto *must* have its Gion scene. (Cue a pair of maiko, in incorrect dress.)

Gion Kobu's history reached its peak of glory in the mid-nineteenth century, when Japan was in serious danger of becoming a European colony. As the shogunate slowly and shamefully collapsed, the angry young samurai of western Japan gathered in Kyoto to scheme, plan, and debate. These men were the architects of their country's future. The revolution that launched Japan into the modern world was hatched in the teahouses of the district, under the watchful protection of the youthful samurai's geisha lovers. This is the bodice-ripping myth of Gion's role in the Meiji Restoration. It is not entirely untrue either. When the angry young samurai replaced the shogunate and took over Japan, many Kyoto geisha followed them to the newly renamed capital, Tokyo.

Their privileged access to the new elite spanned the decades, as the former young samurai grew into elder statesmen and Japan into an empire. Most Japanese people associate the Gion flower-and-willow world with this period over any other. Most historical romances are set in this time, too.

The Gion Kobu hanamachi, then, is a sprightly old dame who wears her proud past with considerable vivacity. It consists of about eighty-three *ochaya* including the famed Ichirikitei, with ninety geiko and twenty maiko. Its school, the Yasaka Nyokoba Academy, is an annex of the Kaburenjo Theatre and was founded in 1873. Like all hanamachi schools, it is a specialist academy, teaching dance, shamisen, percussion, flute, tea ceremony, and calligraphy. There are also options in haiku poetry and *waka*

(or *tanka*). This is a longer poetic form, which is less well-known in the West. It played a crucial part in the development of early Japanese culture; this was the form used for love poetry in the tenth and eleventh centuries, the age of the *Tale of Genji*.

In the past, students entered the academy young, at six years of age. Subsequent changes in education law have made such an early start impossible these days. All Japanese children are required to finish Junior High School (or in British terms, their GCSES). They now start at fifteen or older, to the chagrin of traditionalists. However, even though they may be recognized as maiko and develop into geiko, these achievements are not formally recognized as a proper education. From the Ministry of Education's point of view, these students have failed to go

Left: Noh theater was the established state drama form for centuries. It is stylized, sparse, and hypnotic. Foreigners who fall half asleep at performances are often reassured that this is a good state of mind to enjoy the dreamlike spectacle!

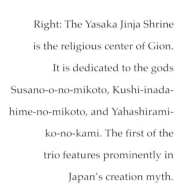

Right: The Yasaka Jinja Shrine is the religious center of Gion. It is dedicated to the gods Susano-o-no-mikoto, Kushi-inada-hime-no-mikoto, and Yahashirami-ko-no-kami. The first of the trio features prominently in Japan's creation myth.

to High School (or get 'A' Levels). This lack of formal diploma status is a great mental burden on many young maiko going through the system in education-conscious Japan. More than a few have dropped out in recent years because of it.

The lack of recognition is bizarre because the teaching staff of the Yasaka Nyokoba Academy are, to put it mildly, of an extraordinary caliber. They include many of the very best artists in Japan, among them dignitaries who have been designated Living National Treasures. This government accolade resembles the French *Legion d'Honneur*, though it is somewhat newer (started in 1955) and conferred only on Japanese nationals.

Of all Gion's treasures, the teaching of Japanese dance (*Nihon buyo*) is the most illustri-

ous. Like most traditional art forms in Japan, *Nihon buyo* is splintered into many styles or schools. The style taught in Gion Kobu is the Inoue School, Japan's most prestigious. The head teacher of the school is Yachiyo Inoue V. (Like kabuki actors, head teachers of artistic styles take the name of their predecessor, with a number suffixed to mark the generation). If the succession is by adoption, the matter is decided by a board of five regents (*koken*). These are local hanamachi dignitaries. [8] All Gion Kobu takes great pride in the Inoue School, especially since it does not operate nationwide; it is unique to their hanamachi. The first person to be designated a Living National Treasure was Inoue Yachiyo IV, grandmother of the present head of the school. There is great pride also in the style's roots, which are to be found in the country's most rarefied theater style—the solemn, hypnotic *aristo* of the Japanese stage, noh drama. Inoue Yachiyo IV is, incidentally, the mother of Katayama Kuroemon, a noh actor of the Kanze school, head of the Japan Noh Association and also a Living National Treasure. Gion Kobu's sense of pride is not merely a matter of snobbery.

Like Germany, Japan is a country with a distinct taste for heraldry. A varied host of crests can be found adorning government buildings, kimono sleeves, and even the offices of *yakuza* groups. Any resemblance to European coats of arms ends there. Japanese crests are stark, monochrome geometric patterns and yet another proof of just how talented the culture is in graphic design. Gion Kobu's crest is a linked circle of eight dots. The dots represent a kind of dumpling called *mitarashi*, an example of the simple fare originally served in the district's teahouses. There are eight of them to represent the eight wards into which the hanamachi was historically divided. In the center is the Chinese character *ko*, "upper."

The other Gion hanamachi, Gion Higashi (East Gion) is much smaller. In fact this is Kyoto's smallest flower town, with eleven *ochaya* containing ten geiko and just five maiko. It lies a only stone's throw away from Gion Kobu, and this is near to the Yasaka Shrine. The two Gion hanamachi parted company in 1886. A series of name changes followed, before the present Gion Kobu-Gion Higashi was adopted in the mid-1940s.

Some Gion Kobu sources take a certain pleasure in looking down their noses at Gion Higashi, and Miyagawa-cho even more so. Snobbery is endemic in the flower-and-willow world, and these two hanamachi were red-light districts before they became geisha quarters.

Nevertheless, Gion Higashi is a working, if miniature, flower town. Like any other hanamachi, its customers are accepted through introductions only. It acts as a full partner with the other hanamachi in joint ventures like the Cherry Dances. It has its *ochaya* and *okiya*, and its *kemban*. In the past, it had its own school, but currently dance classes are given by invited teachers at a rehearsal space provided by the Geiko Association. In this case, the dance style is the Fujima School. Its origins go back to the eighteenth century. Unlike the Inoue School, with its connections to noh drama, the Fujima style takes its cue from kabuki. Its origins are

much more of the people than noh, and to this day kabuki performances are interspersed by cheers and shouts from the actors' loyal fans.

Gion Higashi's crest resembles Gion Kobu's, with the same circle of dumplings. A Chinese character meaning "lower" was removed from the design in the mid-twentieth century, when the hanamachi's organization took on its present shape, centered on the local Association of Teahouse Owners.

Above: Traditional Japanese dance is known as *Nihon buyo*.

Above: Dance practice at a geisha school in Kyoto. Among the teachers are artists formally designated as Living National Treasures.

Ponto-cho

> There's no difference in the snows
> That fall on Fuji's peak,
> And the snows that fall on Ponto-cho,
> They melt and flow the same

So runs a well-loved ballad, *The Snows of Ponto-cho*. The message is egalitarian: rich or poor, people are all the same, from the exalted peak of Japan's sacred mountain to the grittier streets of Kyoto. There is nothing down-market about Ponto-cho, however. This distinguished hanamachi has a history stretching back to the seventeenth century. Its name is also a pointer to its long past. "Ponto" is not a Japanese word in origin. It seems to have come from Portuguese, the word for bridge being the most likely candidate. Portuguese traders and missionaries were active in Japan from the 1540s until the country was shut off by the Tokugawa shogunate in 1635. (The common suffix -cho simply means township. It is pronounced like the beginning of the English word "chosen").

Ponto-cho is the most distinctive of all hanamachi in appearance. The flower town is over the Kamo River from Gion Kobu, and starts immediately north of the Shijo-dori bridge. It consists of a single street, half a kilometer long, backing onto the Kamo. In summer, the guests can be entertained in the open, on elevated platforms perched over the river. There are thirty-seven *ochaya*, with the *kaburenjo* situated in the north. Its geisha arts school, the Kamogawa Academy, is named for the river. Its origins are similar to Gion Kobu's Yasaka Nyokobo, and it teaches the Inoue School dance style. Ponto-cho

has a total of thirty-eight *ochaya* and forty-four geiko. There were seven active maiko as of January 2002. [9]

Rivers and water play an important role in the hanamachi's history. In 1614, the physical shape of the area was formed by the construction of the Takasegawa canal to the west of the Kamo river. The area between the two became Ponto-cho and the early teahouses there depended on trade from the canal. As in Gion, the early teahouses catered to their clients' sexual appetites as well. The teahouses were officially licensed in 1712. During the mid-nineteenth century, while Gion seethed with young samurai plotting the shogunate's downfall, Ponto-cho was the preserve of the pro-government forces at play.

Left: Kyoto geisha carry distinctive traditional umbrellas.

Plovers frequent the banks of the Kamo River in winter. The hanamachi's crest features one, typically stylized.

Miyagawa-cho

The Miyagawa-cho hanamachi district lies back on the east side of the Kamo River, south of Gion Kobu. It is a few minutes walk from the Minamiza theater, and a long connection with kabuki is one of Miyagawa-cho's special features. Another is that this is the one most favored by the locals among the five Kyoto hanamachi. Gion swarms with tourists by day and at night its quiet back streets are lined with black limousines. The passengers are often industrialists and government figures, hailing from outside the city as often as not. Miyagawa-cho, however, is very much a Kyoto preserve and it retains much of the unhurried atmosphere of days gone by. It is fairly large, with thirty-three geiko active in 1999. There were thirty-nine *ochaya* and twenty-four maiko as of April 2002.

A very popular style of TV show in Japan is known as the "wide show." This is an afternoon mix of news, feature spots, and scurrilous gossip about celebrities' lives, with the emphasis wherever possible on the scurrilous gossip. Energetic and accessible, kabuki started out as a form of wide show in the early seventeenth

Below: Japanese traditional performance arts start training their practitioners as early as possible. Six years, six months, and six days was thought the most auspicious time to start off.

century. Its plots were commonly drawn from real-life tragedies and scandals, with courtesans as central characters. It was all a world away from the rarified, contemplative world of noh, with its masked ghosts, aristocrats, and priests. The Floating World was kabuki's cradle. The first kabuki actors were women, of no certain virtue. The shogunate, never amenable to vice without the required paperwork, banned women from the profession in 1629, in vain however. The now male kabuki actors became favorite targets for samurai, priests, and merchants—especially the emerging class of *onnagata* actors, who specialized in women's roles. Traditional Japan had no stigma surrounding homosexuality. In fact, for some of the more macho samurai clans, such as Satsuma in the far southwest, consorting with women was no business for men. As the kabuki world flourished, nearby Miyagawa-cho boomed. Its lodging houses were home to many actors active both onstage and off. *Ochaya* were first licensed in the district in 1751.

Today, the Kyoto flower-and-willow world still maintains close links with kabuki. In many ways, the actors have a great deal in common with the geiko and maiko. Their training is equally rigorous and their world as hedged in with formalities. They form a key group among the patrons of the hanamachi. The link between the two worlds is formalized by the attendance of geiko and maiko at an annual ceremony held at the Minamiza every December. The ceremony is called *kaomise* (showing the face) where kabuki actors formally introduce themselves to the audience, bowing their foreheads to the

floor and begging their favor in quavering, antiquated Japanese. The Kyoto geiko and maiko occupy a gallery, competing with each other with their sumptuous crested kimonos. After the ceremony, the cream of the kabuki performers autograph the maiko's hairpieces, in a formal enactment of what was once, no doubt, a spontaneous piece of fun. The proud Kyoto flower-and-willow world rarely pays such accolades to any living person outside its ranks.

Miyagawa-cho has its academy like the others, the Higashiyama Womens' Academy, teaching the *Wakayagi* ("Young Willow") style of dance. Other hanamachi stream maiko into two types, as mentioned previously. These are the *tachikata*, who concentrate on dance, and the

Above: Scene from the Kamogawa Odori in Kyoto. The performance is by a geiko and younger maiko in praise of the seasons.

jikata, who concentrate on music and singing. Miyagawa-cho is the exception; the Higashiyama Academy prefers all-rounders. [10]

The crest is composed of three circles, celebrating the triple support for the Higashiyama Women's Academy, when it attained government approval. The three groups involved were the local Shinto and Buddhist places of worship, local business, and the Miyagawa-cho hanamachi itself.

Kami Shichiken

Pronounced *kah-mee she-chee-ken*, this is a small cluster of ten *ochaya* with six maiko at present. *Kami* means "upper," *shichi* is "seven," and *ken*, "premises." As the name implies, this hanamachi is set apart from the others, about two kilometers to the northwest. It lies at the end of

Imadegawa-dori, in front of a Shinto shrine called Kitano Tenmangu. Tenmangu shrines cover the length and breadth of Japan. They are dedicated to a deified scholar of the Heian period, Michizane Suguwara (845–903). His heavenly role is to nudge the fates toward providing good exam grades. So, every year the Tenmangu shrines are thronged with students in various stages of nervous collapse; they're going through the crushing pressures of what the Japanese call "examination hell."

Teahouses have existed here longer than in any other Kyoto hanamachi, from the sixteenth century. A massive tea ceremony was held here in 1587 by the shogun Hideyoshi, which filled all seven teahouses from which the area got its name. Hideyoshi was given to grand gestures. He intended to conquer Korea, China, and then India—the whole world, in effect, until the Portuguese arrived in Japan. He rode around brandishing a fan decorated with a map of the three target countries on one side and handy phrases in Chinese, Hindi, and Korean on the other.

Kami Shichiken is a tranquil hanamachi of the quiet back streets. It has strong ties with Shintoism and Buddhism. The landlord of the area is a Buddhist convent, and geiko and maiko practice tea ceremony there even now. The traditional source of custom for the hanamachi is from the locality. The *danna-san* (patrons) are often owners of weaving works which produced cloth for kimonos. Because it has always been a small hanamachi, it does not have a distinct training school as such. Teachers are invited to conduct classes in a rehearsal

Below: A maiko gets advice from an older woman in the street in Gion. The geisha quarters are the last bastions of traditional street life. The maiko is expected to use the appropriate respect language with her elders.

space in the building which also houses the *kemban* (auditing and registration office). This district's crest features dumplings too, ten of them in this case. They commemorate Hideyoshi's jamboree in the sixteenth century; apparently, he was much taken with them.

The six maiko working in Kami Shichiken as of April 2002 offer an interesting example of how professional stage names work in the flower-and-willow world. Their names are Umewaka, Umesono, Umematsu, Umetomo, Umechika, and Naohana. Maiko names are composed of two parts, and one part is usually chosen as a tribute to an Elder Sister or mentor geiko. The *ume* (pronounced "ooh-may") means plum, in this case not the fruit but the delicate white flower, a much treasured sight in Japan. The second part of the name includes, for example *waka* ("youth") and *matsu*, ("pine tree"). Naohana's mentor's name presumably also begins with *nao*; the *hana* means flower.

The Tokyo Hanamachi

Kyoto is a survival from the past, though increasingly demoralized and undermined by modern development. Tokyo belongs entirely to the present. Destroyed by earthquake in 1923, firebombed to the ground in 1945, and relentlessly developed since the sixties, its sense of time is foreshortened. Anything standing for over fifty years is pointed put as old. How could the flower-and-willow world survive in this urban maelstrom? In fact it has done so very well. Power, and hence wealth, are very centralized in Japan. Tokyo is the headquarters of almost all major Japanese firms, and as the economy shrinks, it is shrinking toward the center. The metropolis houses the government, with ministers and their cliques padded with very healthy expense accounts. The tribes of senior bureaucrats are even more powerful and hardly less free-spending. There are even genuine born-and-bred Tokyoites on the city's East

Below: Urban Japan offers a sometimes surreal contrast between traditional and modern, as in this picture.

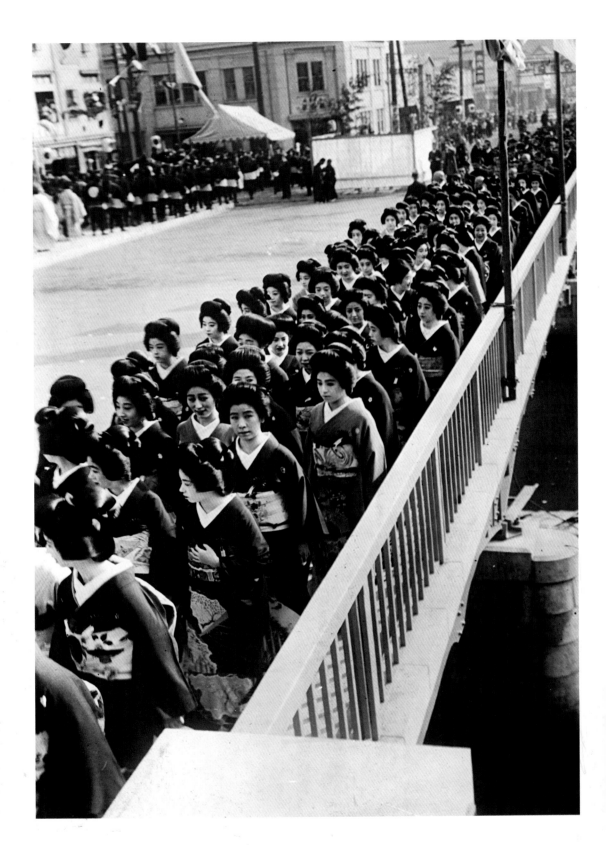

Right: A spectacular parade
of geisha crossing the newly
opened Shimbashi Bridge at its
dedication. They are wearing
formal crested kimonos. Geisha
were a much more common sight
in the early twentieth century
than they are today.

A wig (*katsura*) completes the look. The stress they place on the head causes the geisha to develop a tiny bald spot on the crown.

A wig (katsura) completes the look. The stress they place on the head causes the geisha to develop a tiny bald spot on the crown.

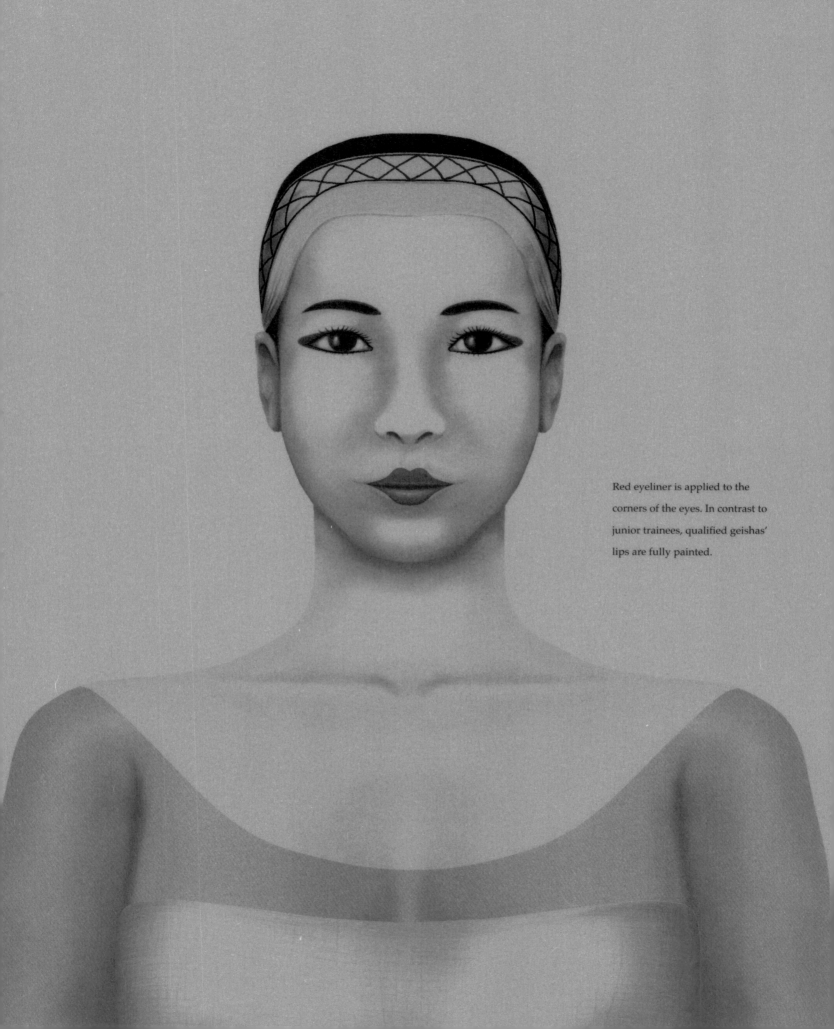

Red eyeliner is applied to the corners of the eyes. In contrast to junior trainees, qualified geishas' lips are fully painted.

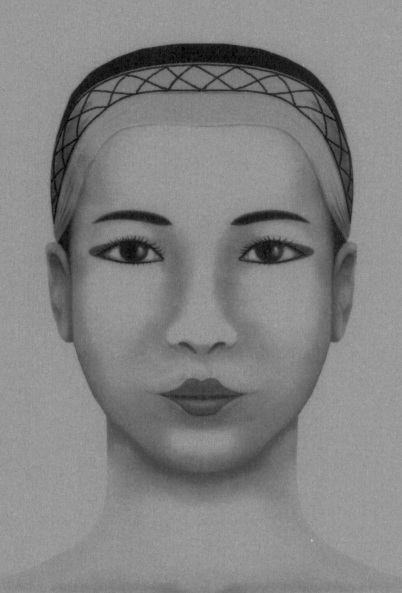

Red eyeliner is applied to the corners of the eyes. In contrast to junior trainees, qualified geishas' lips are fully painted.

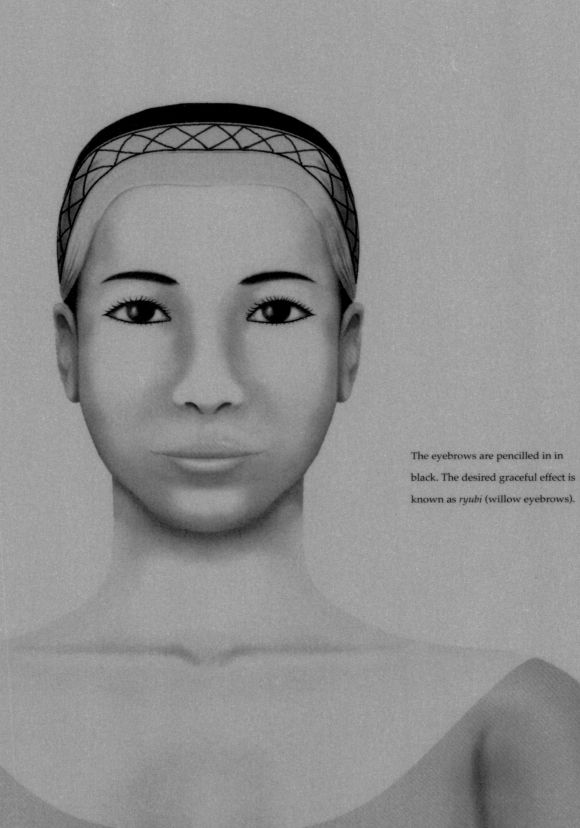

The eyebrows are pencilled in in black. The desired graceful effect is known as *ryubi* (willow eyebrows).

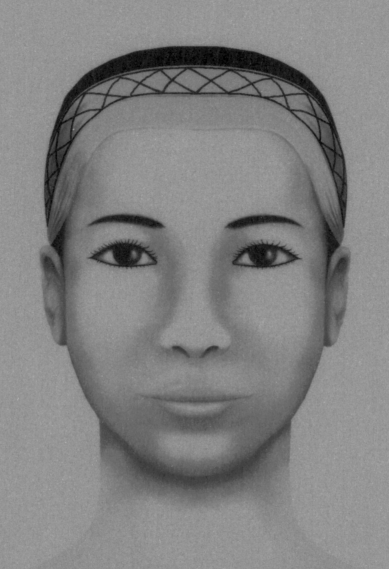

The eyebrows are pencilled in in black. The desired graceful effect is known as *riyhi* (willow eyebrows).

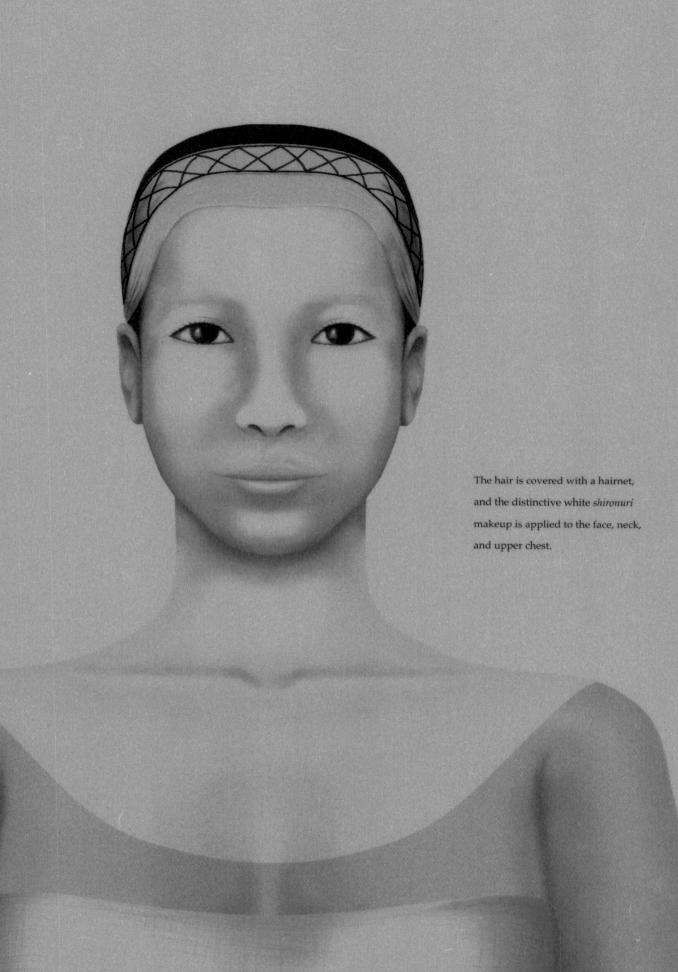

The hair is covered with a hairnet, and the distinctive white *shironuri* makeup is applied to the face, neck, and upper chest.

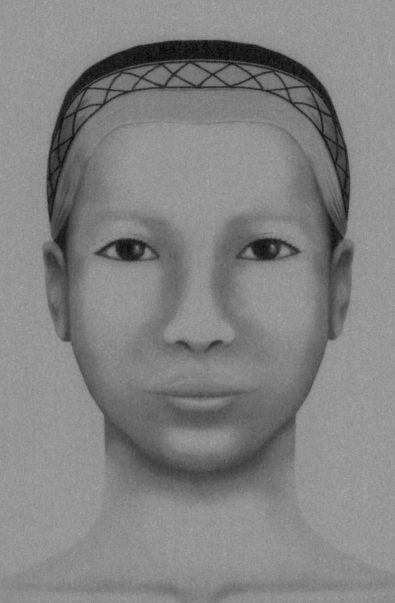

The hair is covered with a hairnet,
and the distinctive white shironuri
makeup is applied to the face, neck,
and upper chest.

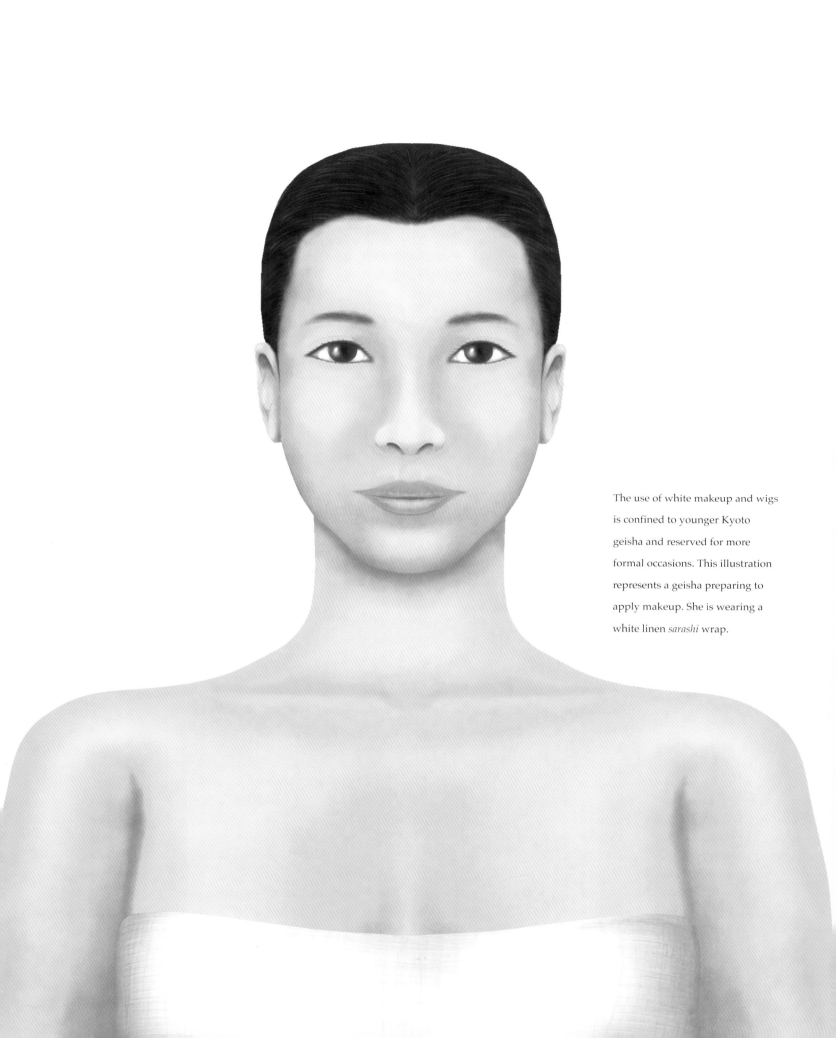

The use of white makeup and wigs is confined to younger Kyoto geisha and reserved for more formal occasions. This illustration represents a geisha preparing to apply makeup. She is wearing a white linen *sarashi* wrap.

side who maintain decades-old relationships with geisha districts, and spend their own companies' expense accounts doing so.

Unlike Kyoto, the Tokyo flower-and-willow world is centered on *ryotei*; these are very high-class traditional restaurants. *Okiya* are usually referred to as geisha houses. Overall, the key is a good deal lower than in Kyoto, and it has been so right throughout the history of the profession. Geisha are not a main tourist attraction here, which is all to the good. Tourists do not clutter the streets snapping maiko, pretend or otherwise. In fact maiko do not exist here; apprentices are called *hangyoku* ("half-fee") and do not have a distinctive costume. Kimonos are more conservative, the white face paint absent. The yearly calendar of events is less Byzantine than Kyoto, closer to the average citizen's round of New Year, Setsubun festival in February, cherry blossom viewing in April, moon viewing in October, and so on. The same sense of exclusivity and expense prevails, however, and of course the sense of *iki*. The geisha world was, after all, born in old Edo. While just as sophisticated and varied as the Kyoto flower-and-willow world, it is less ritualized, less insulated from the outside world. It also retains something more of the old earthiness, though its sense of *hauteur* belongs to a world-class metropolis.

For the last century or so, the history of the Tokyo hanamachi has revolved around the varying fortunes of the Shimbashi, Akasaka, and Asakusa geisha quarters.

The history of the Tokyo hanamachi has revolved around the varying fortunes of the Shimbashi, Akasaka, and Yanagimachi geisha quarters.

Shimbashi

Shimbashi is currently the most successful of Tokyo hanamachi. It lies between the Ginza district and Tokyo Bay. This was where the angry young samurai from Kyoto went for relaxation after the move of the capital from Kyoto to Edo (renamed Tokyo). Many of the faces there were familiar from Kyoto. These men were imperial loyalists, with a deep sense of entitlement to power. They were also rich and free-spending patrons to the geisha. At the turn of the century, however, the growing power of democratic politics in Japan shifted the center of the political world toward Akasaka, home of the national parliament, Diet. The Shimbashi hanamachi began to cater more to the business elite. It still retained a very exclusive aura, however, and was used to entertain visiting dignitaries like Richard Nixon and Jean-Paul Sartre. Shimbashi Embujo is the geisha theatre, and *Azuma Odori* (Dances of the East) in May is the main event.

Two developments in the 1990s helped Shimbashi retain its status in Tokyo. The first was the decline of the equally classy Yanagibashi district due to property development and the westward shift in Tokyo's development. The other was the scourging of the Akasaka hanamachi through public outrage at the amount of taxpayers' money being spent there by politicians. The ambience is relatively sedate and homely.

Akasaka

Politics is the lifeblood of this hanamachi, set close to the national parliament, the Diet. The Akasaka *ryotei* are the scene of Japan's real politics, in a sense. For Diet politicians, speeches in the parliament are very much a formality. British residents of Japan, looking for the wit and rowdiness of the English parliament, will look in vain. The dry, pre-scripted question-and-answer sessions are not for the easily bored. Eloquence is suspect in Japan, even in politicians. It smacks of sophistry, as do grand ideas.

Politics, like every other business of importance, is conducted face to face, over flasks of sake and behind closed doors. Preferably behind the closed doors of an Akasaka *ryotei*; the walls have ears here, too, of course, but they never speak. Just as in revolutionary Kyoto, the geisha never divulge what they hear; to do so would be suicidal for their business. Even so, the hanamachi is in trouble.

Gift giving is a deeply rooted part of Japanese life, an important way of maintaining good relations with friends and colleagues. It is common in politics and the line between gifts and bribes has never been really made clear. High-class entertaining was traditionally seen as an excellent way to smooth projects through with other politicians, bureaucrats, and industrialists. Things got quite out of hand during the bubble period in the 1980s. In 1998, though, the public really boiled over when the media exposed Ministry of Finance officials being "entertained" by Dai-Ichi Kangyo Bank in a *no-pan shabu-shabu* restaurant. This now-infamous establishment features miniskirted waitresses with nothing on underneath. Enough was enough. A raft of legislation limiting entertainment perks for bureaucrats was passed, which unleashed a financial drought on both sleazier venues and the Akasaka hanamachi. There are now thirteen under-frequented *ryotei*.[11]

The atmosphere of the Akasaka geisha district is even more exclusive but less formal than Shimbashi. Japanese politics operates on a gerrymander system. Rural voters elect more representatives per head than their urban cousins. Consequently, the politicians are often country bumpkins compared to the traditional men of *tsu*. Asakusa geisha have a reputation for being both friendlier and raunchier than in Shimbashi, though their standards of Japanese dance are not quite so high.

Asakusa

There are three other major hanamachi active in Tokyo: Kagurazaka, Yoshicho, and Asakusa. Of

Left: Maiko in Kyoto. As a rule of thumb, the more colorful they are, the more junior.

these, Asakusa is the most notable. Rather like Miyagawa-cho in Kyoto, it is more down-to-earth, and a favorite haunt for natives of Tokyo. With its East Asian equivalent of Cockney sparrows and loveable rogues, the whole district occupies a place in Japanese hearts rather like the East End of London for the English. It has very strong traditional connections with the *taikomochi* male geisha tradition, and with the related craft of *rakugo* storytelling. It can be relatively accessible, too.

The Asakusa *kemban*, for example, hosts regular meetings of its "Swings" club. It is not salacious—the name is a play on a variant reading for the character *iki* and it promotes an appreciation of geisha and related performance styles. It is especially aimed at the young. Entrance fees, at 10,000 Yen for students and 15,000 Yen for others, may not seem cheap but they are a fraction of normal hanamachi rates and new faces are welcome. The program typically includes *rakugo* storytelling, workshops on how to wear kimonos, etiquette, *taikomochi* performance, and Japanese dance by geisha. It is hard to imagine such a no-frills approach in Shimbashi or Akasaka, let alone Gion Kobu.

Yanagibashi

Yanagibashi is the dead star of the Tokyo flower-and-willow world. Like Kyoto's Ponto-cho, it was a riverine geisha district, situated by gardens on the banks of the broad Sumida River. An invitation to one of its high-class restaurants to watch the summer fireworks festival was a mark of having truly arrived in the

Regional Hanamachi

metropolis. There were pleasure boats in summer, too. The venerable *taikomochi* Tamasuke Yugentei remembers these boats as magical, over sixty years later. He was especially taken with pleasure cruises for a single geisha and guest; the captain would be paid to leave the couple, mooring the craft at a tree called "the Pine of Head-to-Toe Success." The bubble period of the 1980s put paid to Yanagibashi's riverside gardens and the recession and Tokyo's westward drift eventually put paid to the hanamachi too. It faded out just before the millennium.

Every major Japanese city has its hanamachi, though many of them are in danger of going the way of Yanagibashi. Fukuoka, in the southern island of Kyushu, seems one of the likeliest to survive. It enjoys at least an informal level of contact with Gion Kobu, whose geiko and maiko have performed there. Geisha survive even in the city of Osaka, a massive gray metropolis whose colorful, energetic inhabitants happily ignore every Japanese tradition which might threaten to slow down business. In some

Above: A market street in the colorful Asakusa district of Tokyo. Blossoming cherry tree branches are displayed above the shops. The gritty, earthy quality of Asakusa life is still widely valued. The Asakusa hanamachi helps to preserve the area's down-to-earth character.

Far left: Geisha taking part in a festival procession.

places, such as Kanazawa on the Sea of Japan coast, the decline has been stemmed in part by local government help. As Leslie Downer points out, however, this involves a "Faustian pact" with the local authorities: since public money is being used, rehearsals have to be opened to the public. The hanamachi's proud, cat-like independence disappears along with its mystique. Most regional hanamachi are as shy of publicity as the Kyoto geisha quarters.

Geisha and the Traditional Japanese Arts

Geisha are artists first and foremost. No other single profession requires quite the range of hands-on expertise in traditional Japanese arts as is expected of a fully-fledged Kyoto geiko. Yet there is no single art form which is uniquely the flower-and-willow world's very own. Japanese dance, tea ceremony, flower arranging,

and calligraphy all have their practitioners in the broader world outside. Tea ceremony and flower arranging in particular are practiced by literally millions of people (the number of tea ceremony students is estimated at six million nationwide). Nowadays, these accomplishments are seen as especially desirable in young women who plan to get married. They offer a primer in the poise, calm, and patience that are expected of the virtuous Japanese wife. Marriage rates are nosediving at present. Young Japanese women are backing away, *forte con brio*, from the ornamental-flower-cum-domestic-caretaker role. Yet they continue to practice flower arranging and tea. They now claim the poise, calm, and patience for themselves, not for some corporate samurai husband-to-be.

The geisha arts are not the exclusive property of the flower-and-willow world. The way in which they cover them all them certainly is. In Chapter Four we will examine in more detail

Right: An attendant assists an actor with costume and makeup for a performance as a geisha, a traditional female role.

Above left: A quintessential Japanese pleasure: a hot spring in the southern island of Kyushu. Bathing was segregated in the 1870s as a concession to outraged Western tourists.

Below left: A traditional ensemble (from left to right): the *taiko*, the shamisen and the *kotsuzumi*. Child geisha in Tokyo were known as *hangyoku* ("half-jewel"), meaning that their party fee was half that of an adult performer's.

the arts especially associated with geisha—Japanese dance and shamisen playing. In order to get a feel for the entire area, however, we will begin by looking at the most popular of the arts which geisha also cover in their training. As it introduces us to the thinking behind these practices, we shall look at one of them here in some length: tea ceremony.

Tea Ceremony (*Sado*)

Tea ceremony has been memorably described by Lesley Downer as "somewhere between tai chi and the Roman Catholic mass, but on a very small, intimate scale." [12] A group of people, ideally four, meet in a small tatami-floored room and drink *maccha*, a frothy, vivid green tea which is quite bitter. This is the baldest possible summary of events. The tea ceremony is a kind of philosophical microcosm. The tea ceremony room is a tiny space in which Japan's profoundest theories of aesthetic and religious truth are deployed and enacted.

In Japanese the tea ceremony is called *sado*, which means "the Way of Tea." "Way" here does not mean method; it means way as in "road," quite literally. The road is long. It requires years of patient practice to traverse it to the very end. Every move is completely prescribed—the ladle is placed precisely this distance from the lip of the urn, the hand cloth is folded just so and placed exactly there and in no other place. As the years pass, second nature slowly becomes first nature. The moment arrives, and the practitioner is free. The rules have evaporated but there is no obvious outward change.

Zen Buddhism is now so well-known in the West that the connections hardly need pointing out. Every waking moment of the Zen novice's life is as rigidly controlled as a tea ceremony. The mind is concentrated on one of the famous *koan* or Zen riddles: "I saw my beloved in a corner of the sky" for example. [13] The despairing, exhausted novice is "a mosquito trying to bite a lump of iron." The breakthrough arrives, in this case *satori* or enlightenment, and the novice "awakes." Again, the person's outward life need change not a jot. A Zen adept can be a high school teacher just as easily as a monk.

What is the point of the exercise? It is not religious in the Western sense of acquiring virtue or salvation. Rather, one loses something:

Below: Tea ceremony is a kind of philosophical microcosm. Its aesthetic is called *wabi*, implying a love of plain, timeworn things.

"The 'observing self' is eliminated; a man 'loses himself,' that is, he ceases to be a spectator of his acts'…Nothing remains but the goal and the act that accomplishes it. [14]

The goal itself is of no great concern; Japanese culture has never been very strong on defining destinations; the journey itself is the focus.

The names of a number of Japanese arts end with –do (way), shodo (calligraphy), kado (flower arranging), kyudo (archery), and of course judo and other martial arts like aikido. They all share this sense of perfectionism. They all act as pathways into everyday life for the rarified ideas of Zen Buddhism. The fully committed geisha approaches every aspect of her craft with great seriousness of purpose—even the art of trivial conversation (which has a name: wajutsu).

The design of the tea ceremony room is resolutely simple. The room is essentially bare tatami matting. A small vacancy in the floor holds the charcoal fire for warming the water. A rustic pillar supports the equally plain ceiling. An alcove holds a flower arrangement and a hanging scroll, with some calligraphy and perhaps a picture painted on it. The tea ceremony aesthetic is founded on the idea of wabi. This means a love for the plain, the quiet, the unpatterned; natural materials, unadorned. Wabi especially values the used over the new, and treasures traces of use on old artifacts. The look of the hanamachi teahouse room is directly derived from the tea ceremony room.

The full-scale tea ceremony in the purpose-built tea ceremony house is now a rather rare

event in Japan. Many colleges, schools, and other institutions, as well as some well-off private houses have a tea ceremony room, however. Typically, when the guests first enter the room, they are welcomed by the host and admire the alcove (tokonoma) with its scroll and flower arrangement. The scroll will typically be inscribed with a verse or saying related to Buddhism. They then sit formally, on the floor with their legs tucked beneath them. The host boils the water, cleans and wipes the tea bowl, then pours and whisks the tea and offers it ceremonially to the guests. The precise manner in which this is done depends on which of the tea

Above: The tea room is the direct ancestor of the ochaya party space.

ceremony's many schools is being practiced. The tea bowls may look very plain to the Western eye, but they are often extremely expensive works of art in themselves. These too are ceremoniously appreciated by the guests, before drinking. Like everything else in tea ceremony, conversation is highly stylized. Traditional confectionery is served, to offset the bitterness of the green tea. The fire contains scented woods. Properly done, the experience is as satisfying to the spirit as it is prosaic in description.

Central to the enjoyment of the tea ceremony is the interplay of textures, colors, and art forms such as architecture, pottery, calligraphy, flower arrangement, and the culinary arts. While Japanese clothing is not always worn, textiles are a feature of any formal tea ceremony. Every aspect of the room and the clothing is

Above right : A richly costumed performer enacts the tea ceremony.

Below right : A geisha pours tea against a backdrop of spectacular flower arrangements.

carefully chosen to match the season. The art form was first perfected by Japan's greatest aesthetician, Sen no Rikyu (1522–1591). He also played a crucial role in the development of flower arranging (*ikebana*).

Ikebana (Flower Arranging)

The second of the great arts with huge popularity is *ikebana* ("flowers made to live"). It is also known as *kado* ("the Way of Flowers"), and so it shares with tea ceremony the idea of spiritual training. Accomplished practitioners of *ikebana* create pristine works of art, crystalline miniature worlds which draw the viewer deep into their silent hearts. *Ikebana* enacts the fundamental axiom of the Japanese aesthetic: that less is more. It expresses that aesthetic through its most fundamental drive: the urge to asymmetry. *Ikebana* is also of Buddhist origin. It is a refinement of Buddhist flower offerings that began in the fifteenth century. Like all the arts, it developed many schools and styles. It is completely different from Western flower arranging as its sense of spatiality includes empty space and the spaces between the branches. In the most popular style, called *shoka*, arrangements of three main branches represent the traditional East Asian trinity of heaven, humanity, and earth. As with tea ceremony, there is a layer of symbolism based on yin-yang ideas.

The style most closely associated with tea ceremony is an austere form which grew out of the *nageire* style developed by Sen no Rikyu in the sixteenth century. His style was studiously casual. *Nageire* means to cast or fling something into a container. In contrast with earlier, more elaborate arrangements, this could consist of a single, exquisitely displayed flower. Hideyoshi was a flamboyant shogun of the time and was the host of Kami Shichiken's mammoth tea ceremony. The story goes that he heard Sen no Rikyu's tea ceremony house in Kyoto boasted a beautiful garden of deep purple morning glory. He sent the tea master a note, inviting himself the next day. He passed through the gate—the garden was bare. Every stem had been cut. Angrily, he swept into the tea house. In a vase in the alcove lay a single, incandescent morning glory.

Calligraphy

Calligraphy is also a way, –*shodo*, the way of writing. It is perhaps the most difficult of Japanese arts for Westerners to appreciate. Partly this is because the writing systems are so very different. Yet Arabic calligraphy is

Left: "Less is more" and "asymmetry, not symmetry" as exemplified in a bonsai tree.

Right: *Ikebana* has a mass following in modern Japan.

incomprehensible but visually beautiful even to the person who doesn't read the language. We may not know the names, but the sinuous *Naskh* style or the solemn, regular blocks of *Kufic* script are immediately accessible as works of art. By contrast, when approaching the curving smudges or splashy angular lines that make up East Asian calligraphy, it can sometimes be an unsettling experience for the Western observer. Unquestionably one is looking at a work of extreme beauty but what we lack is any frame of reference from which to approach it.

East Asian calligraphy is essentially a form of visual music. The artist approaches the Chinese character like a cellist would a score. The aim is balance of composition, rhythm, delicacy or strength, and above all *aji*—the taste of the artist's personality expressed in the work. The composition is executed in a few seconds and that is that. There is no going back over it. The artist's control of breathing, physical balance, and feeling are all contained in the result. The onlooker follows the event as it happened, stroke by stroke, feeling to some degree at least what the artist felt. The work of calligraphy captures a unique moment. The approach is very personal. There is no need for the result to be conventionally legible. The only legible writing surviving from one of Japan's most famous calligraphers is a note asking a friend for some money. [15] The calligraphy style most closely associated with the tea ceremony is known as *bokuseki* ("ink traces"). As the name suggests, it is austere. It is normally the work of a master and contains a Buddhist proverb.

Japanese calligraphy impacts on the flower-and-willow world in a number of ways. Along with the *ikebana* flower arrangement, the scroll of calligraphy is the centerpiece of the room where parties are held. The scroll will normally be changed for each customer. Also, geisha handwriting appears on the ceremonial envelopes which are exchanged at so many Japanese formal occasions. From antiquity, people have been judged on their handwriting in every country touched by Chinese written culture. A proper geisha's script should be legible, expressive, and exquisite.

The flower-and-willow world and the traditional Japanese arts form a seamless, inseparable whole. Millions of Japanese practice tea ceremony. The number of people who practice it in a living community, that wears traditional clothes every day and that speaks Japanese with all the old finesse, can be numbered in the hundreds. They are all in the geisha community or closely linked to it.

Left: A geisha carrying a paper umbrella walks through the Heian Gardens in Kyoto

CHAPTER 2
the history of the geisha

In the primal past, Japan was saved through dance and geisha have long memories.

Right: This woman is wearing a strongly-patterned version of the traditional Heian-period court lady's multi-layered kimono.

Far right: In Japan's creation myth, the Sun Goddess Amaterasu-o-mikami hid herself from the world in a cave when insulted by her brother. This rather prim rendition is from the series *Dai nippon meisho Kagami* ("A Mirror of Famous Generals").

大日本名将鑑

天照皇大神天の巌戸に隠れさせ
たまひ世の中常闇のおゝくらく
なれば八百萬の神たち巌戸の
前に集ひ神いさめの神楽を奏
し一百女命舞ひ遊ばれゝど天神
扉をすこし開きぬひてアゝ面白
やとの給ふを手力雄命其扉を
とつて投みひ遥かふ飛て信ふれ
取て投みひ遥かふ飛て信ふれ
止る依て戸隠明神と申し奉る

届明治十五年二月十六日
根津宮永町三丁五十二番地
神田区元柳原町三番地二十
出板　秘津忠次郎
画工　月岡米次郎

芳年

The Sun Goddess Amaterasu-o-mikami had reason to be incensed by her outrageous brother, the trickster god Susano-o-no-mikoto. Not only had he broken down the divisions between her rice fields but he had stolen into her palace, where "he secretly voided excrement." Worse was to come. Spotting Amaterasu weaving garments in her sacred hall, he broke a hole in the roof and flung in a "heavenly piebald horse" which "he had flayed with a backward flaying." Amaterasu took refuge in a cave, casting the Central Land of Fertile Reed-plains (Japan, of course) into darkness. Consternation ensued until finally:

> Ama-no-uzume-no-mikoto, ancestress of the Sarume Chieftain, took in her hand a spear wreathed with Eulalia grass, and standing before the door of the Rock-cave of Heaven, skilfully performed a mimic dance… Now Amaterasu heard this and said, 'Since I have shut myself up in the Rock-cave, there ought surely to be continual night in the Central Land of Fertile Reed-plains. How then can Ama-no-uzume-no-mikoto be so jolly?' So with her august hand, she opened for a narrow space the Rock-door and peeped out. Then Ta-jikara-o-no-kami forthwith took Amaterasu by the hand and led her out. [16]

We need not describe in detail the exact nature of the "mimic dance" performed by Ama-no-uzume, spear in hand. Japanese *manga* cartoonists have beaten us to it, leaving little enough to the imagination. In the primal past, Japan was saved through dance and geisha have long memories. When Ponto-cho maiko vow obedience to their Older Sisters over sacred cups of sake, the scroll displayed in the alcove shows the figure of Amaterasu. The trickster god Susano-o is worshipped to this day at the Yasaka Shrine in Gion.

The legend of Amaterasu was written down in 720 in the *Nihon shoki* ("Chronicles of Japan"). Buddhism had been accepted in the mid-sixth century and with it came its scriptures written in classical Chinese, the Latin of the Far East. Japan had its first permanent capital city—Nara, a solemn city of massive Chinese-style temples just south of modern Kyoto. Here, Japanese was written down for the first time, giving us a first glimpse into the hearts of mortals rather than gods. The monumental work of the time was the *Manyoshu* ("A Collection of Myriad Leaves"), a huge anthology of poetry with themes of love and longing. A man journeying to Nara looks into the sea:

> As deeply do I
> think of my wife
> who swayed toward me in sleep
> like the lithe seaweed.
> Yet few were the nights
> we had slept together
> before we were parted
> like crawling vines uncurled.

Even at this remote stage of Japanese history, female entertainers were active. They were called *saburuko* ("serving girls") and they were wanderers whose families had been displaced because of factional struggles in the late 600s.

Even at this remote stage of Japanese history, female entertainers were active.

Some simply sold their bodies in order to survive. Others, more fortunate or from more educated backgrounds, made their way entertaining at aristocratic gatherings.

Heian Kyoto: The Making of a Courtly Love Tradition

In 794 the imperial court moved to the newly founded capital, Heian-kyo, also known as Kyoto. Here a culture grew up which took the poetic forms and the romantic outlook of the *Manyoshu* to the farthest possible extremes. Heian-period Kyoto was the graceful capital of a country at peace. It became the home of a tiny, ultra-aesthetic noble elite who dedicated themselves to the pursuit of refined hedonism. The most taxing pursuit for the noblemen was playing a form of ritual kickball. They were also kept busy with other affairs, like attending incense parties and guessing the composition of the scent. They were active in mixing their own fragrances too and moon viewing was popular. Sometimes, being nobles, they had to line up as cavalry for inspection. Captains' reports survive to tell us what happened. They fell off their horses!

For the Heian nobleman, the pursuit of desire was the only truly serious object in life. The object of desire was the Heian noblewoman, a fabulous creature wrapped in multi-layered robes, with a bolt of jet-black tresses shooting to the floor.

She was usually confined to her mansion, though on occasion she attended Buddhist ceremonies in a closed carriage. Her wide

sleeves trailed out of the latticed windows, sending the men into a frenzy. Contact between the sexes was by means of the thirty-one-syllable *waka* poem, pressed into the hand of a maid or other go-between. It was the poem that was crucial—the form, the handwriting, the exquisiteness of the paper. If the poems exchanged were appealing enough, the man stole in at

Above: A *shirabyoshi* dancer in formal male court clothes of the Heian era preparing to dance. She wears the *eboshi* hat of a high official; the painted eyebrows on her forehead called "moth eyebrows" after the silk moth. *Shirabyoshi* were connected with female shamanism.

Right: A scene from *The Tale of Genji*, the world's first psychological novel and a key primer in the ultra-aesthetic mentality of the Heian-period elite. It was written by Murasaki Shikibu around the year 1000, and is still recognized as the greatest single masterpiece of Japanese literature.

night to the lady's chamber, and the relationship was consummated. Sex itself seems to have been the least important part of the whole process. The men had access to all kinds of partners—multiple wives, concubines, maids, and prostitutes. The women, too, could take numerous lovers. Heian romance was more like an aesthetic extreme sport. The thrill of entering a lady's bed, or of welcoming a lover, was like a skydiver's pleasure in falling with perfect balance. Anyone can simply jump out of a plane.

The tiny Heian circle of women writers produced astounding literature like *The Pillow Book of Sei Shonagon* and *The Tale of Genji*, the world's first novel. It was written by Murasaki Shikibu around the year 1000. The Shining Prince Genji

is the Hamlet and Heathcliff of Japanese literature, an aristocratic lover of innumerable women including a concubine of the emperor himself. Yet he is tortured by the impossibility of his quest for perfect beauty, and more than a little influenced by the pessimistic Buddhism of his day.

The role of Prince Genji is buried deep in the Japanese male psyche. It is often deeply concealed beneath a façade of curt respectability. Part of a geisha's task is to somehow transport men from everyday life to the world of the Shining Prince. They can even be tough about it. A legendary ninth-century beauty, the writer Ono no Komachi, tested a pining lover by making him sleep outside her window for a hundred nights. A thousand years later, the geiko Iwasaki Mineko tested the love of her life in a similar way in 1960s Kyoto:

> "If you really love me then I want you to prove it. Remember the poet Ono no Komachi? How she made Officer Fukakusa visit her for one hundred nights before she would give him her hand? Well, I want you to visit Gion Kobu every night for the next three years. Every night. Without exception...If you complete this task we can talk again." [17]

He did, and she accepted him. Poor Officer Fukukawa was not so fortunate. Legend has it that he passed away on the ninety-ninth night.

An Age of Iron: 1100–1600

Far from the capital's incense parties and love poetry lived the clans of the east and north. These were tough frontier people, rolling back the indigenous Ainu while learning to survive the grim winters of northern Honshu. As control from Kyoto loosened, they began fighting amongst themselves. When it lapsed altogether, the victors launched for the center, and power. The aristocracy didn't stand a chance. By 1183, Kyoto was in the hands of eastern warriors, the Minamoto clan. An age of iron had begun.

The romantic hero of the age was Minamoto no Yoshitsune, younger brother of the new shogun Minamoto no Yoshinaka. The *beau ideal* was now of sterner cast. Yoshitsune won his spurs in a daring charge which smashed the

rival Taira clan. Like many successful generals, he fell under suspicion. He was outlawed by his brother, and fled as a hunted fugitive. His wanderings were immortalized in *The Tale of Heike,* which celebrated the faithfulness of his retainers, and the beauty of his lovers.

The heroine was Yoshitsune's favorite concubine, Shizuka Gozen, a dancer with shamanistic powers. She exemplifies the figure of the *shirabyoshi*, a remote ancestor of the geisha. *Shirabyoshi* emerged as dancers and courtesans in the mid-Heian period, but reached the peak of their popularity from the twelfth to the sixteenth centuries. They were highly skilled and highly provocative. They wore men's white clothing, and their dances were both sacred and erotic. Today, their descendants can be found serving as altar

Left: Minamoto no Yoshitsune was the archetype of the chivalrous warrior. His campaigning enabled his brother Yoritomo to become shogun in 1185, though he himself ended his life as a hunted fugitive. The warrior class evolved over time into the samurai.

attendants at Shinto shrines. Their patrons included the old aristocratic families like the Fujiwara, and their tougher samurai successors. Many of them came from upper-class families who had run out of luck in the wars which were gradually becoming endemic throughout the country. When Yoshitsune was captured and executed, Shizuka Gozen entered a Buddhist convent. She was eighteen years old.

After the fall of the nobility, Japan very slowly dissolved into armed anarchy. The emperors struggled to claw back real power, sometimes with brief success. The shogunate proved strong enough to see off two Mongol invasions, but it couldn't pay the troops, now fully-fledged samurai. It collapsed in 1333. A revived government under the Ashikaga family failed to halt the drift into civil war. In the Onin War of the late 1460s, the front line ran right through Kyoto. The old imperial capital, with its myriad temples and palaces, was laid waste.

The following century and a half is remembered as the Warring States period. Warlords roamed the land, scourging the defenceless peasantry. *Shirabyoshi* dancers entertained the elite, but the concerns of ordinary women were avoiding starvation, looting, and rape. People felt abandoned by heaven. They called their world the *ukiyo*, the floating world of misery, with nothing in it to depend upon. A large part of Japan's obsession with order comes from the horrific experiences of this time. Yet the dream of Heian culture and sophistication never quite died out.

Japan's middle ages were when the most distinctively Japanese culture was laid down.

After the fall of the nobility, Japan very slowly dissolved into armed anarchy.

The more violent the times, the more refined the arts became. The ultra-urbane *nageire* flower arranging style, for example, developed in Kyoto as the city was burning in the Onin War. All the raw elements of geisha craft came out of this cauldron.

Heian etiquette was a hugely elaborate, unwritten ritual code. It governed matters like the required color combinations for robes in each of twenty-four separate annual seasons. The etiquette developed by the samurai was called the *Ogasawara* style, after the member of the Minamoto clan who developed it in the fourteenth century. This code covered "manners in times of peace and campaign strategy in times of war." It stipulated behavior when entering tatami rooms, how to bow on doing so, where to place one's feet when walking to one's seat, and where exactly to sit in relation to other people in the room. Even today, when older Japanese want to relax, they say to each other "Let's dispense with the Ogasawara School." The one community where it retains its full rigor is the flower-and-willow world.

Tea ceremony was the crucial driving force in the development of the whole tatami environment. Eight years after the Minamoto warriors took Kyoto in 1193, a monk called Eisai returned from study in China. He brought two things with him: Zen Buddhism and Chinese tea ceremony. Zen found a ready audience among the warrior class. The conscious, commentating mind is a deadly distraction in hand-to-hand combat. The Zen adept learns how to discard the conscious mind.

Left: *The Gion District* by Yoshitoshi
Tsukioka. Rikiya, a young hero of
the epic drama *Chuushingura*,
enters the Ichiriki teahouse in
Kyoto, where his father is plotting
to avenge the death of their master.
The title of the epic literally trans-
lates as "A Storehouse of Faithful
Retainers," and the conspirators
remain heroic figures to this day.
The Ichiriki teahouse still operates,
and the connection with
Chuushingura is an essential compo-
nent of its extraordinary cachet.

Right: *The Courtesan Takao of Miura-ya Displaying New Bedclothes*, a woodblock by Kitagawa Tsukimaro. The licensed pleasure quarters of the Tokugawa shogunate became the scene of a hyperactive, commercialized version of Heian-period decadence.

Tea ceremony seems a less likely candidate for the attentions of the warrior, however. It seems especially so from the modern viewpoint, where tea is mainly an accomplishment for the young lady (or geisha) of polite upbringing. Yet it flourished among warriors as much as monks. Tea drinking became widespread in the early 1200s, but it was only under the extremely violent conditions of the fifteenth and sixteenth centuries that it reached its fully developed form as a meeting place for the arts.

For his retirement, the shogun of the Onin War, Ashikaga Yoshimasa, settled in a luxurious Kyoto villa called the Silver Pavilion, in 1483. His curator of Chinese artworks, a tea master called Murata Shoko, was the first to develop the humble tea ceremony room, a mere four-and-a-half tatami mats in size. He was also the first to add calligraphy to the mix, hanging scrolls containing Buddhist sayings. Trade with China was now open again, and a group of wealthy merchants near Osaka were receptive

to his teachings. This "warehouse school" produced Sen no Rikyu, the ultimate master of the "Way of Tea."

Sen no Rikyu transformed the tea ceremony. He did away with the gorgeous bowls and implements of the Chinese style, and put humble Japanese earthenware in their place. His four-and-a-half-mat tea huts were models of restraint. The tea hut, in turn, inspired the style of architecture that provides the model for the *ochaya*, *okiya*, and *ryotei* alike. Unlike most Japanese people these days, geisha spend most of their working lives in this environment and often live in it too. Rikyu developed the equally understated *nageire* flower arrangement style to complement the spare tatami spaces. His style was the epitome of *wabi*.

Sixteenth-century tea ceremony was not a finishing school for young ladies. It was effectively politics by other means and Sen no Rikyu was a political player of the highest order:

Tea was a ritual of total peace. Teahuts and rooms became the antipodes of war and violence. They were known to be the only places where members of the leading samurai class left their swords outside…As far as we know, no one has ever been assassinated in a tearoom. [18]

The tea master's role as host of the political gathering finds expression again and again in the flower-and-willow world, from nineteenth-century Gion with its disaffected samurai, to twenty-first-century Akasaka with its scheming politicos.

The wars reached a crescendo during Sen no Rikyu's lifetime. The flamboyant warlord Toyotomi Hideyoshi finally united Japan in 1590. His great tea ceremony in Kami Shichiken was a symbol of his political power. He invited all *wabi* people, rich and poor, to prove the extent of his reach. On display were tea bowls, implements, and scrolls seized from his enemies to symbolize their defeat, or offered by tributaries to prove their submission.

Hideyoshi's attacks on Korea in the 1590s were bloodstained failures, but the returning troops brought with them potters who developed some of Japan's most prized tea wares, including Satsuma, Arita, and Hagi. The mixture of carnage and high culture was typical of the time. Even noh drama was pressed into service. Wandering troupes were by now so popular that commoners paid handsomely to perform onstage. Gion Kobu geisha likewise spend vast sums mounting public performances like the Cherry Dance, their

steps echoing the noh "art of walking" they have learned at the Inoue School. Hideyoshi wrote ten noh plays, starring himself. Noh was still the official state drama of Japan when Admiral Perry sailed into Tokyo Bay in 1853.

Above: *The Sun of Advancement* by Yoshitoshi. This is from a kabuki series called *Seven Brilliant Stars* and shows the actor Bando Hikasaburo as the sixteenth century warlord Hideyoshi.

Right: On his rise to supreme power, Tokugawa Ieyasu, founder of the Tokugawa shogunate, made many enemies. Dissatisfied with the results of his alliance with Ieyasu, Sanada Yukimura rebelled against him. During the seige of Osaka in 1615 he hid in a lotus pond and attempted to assassinate him. The attempt failed, Yukimura escaped, but was killed shortly afterward. A gray but much needed peace descended on the country thereafter.

With the country on the road to being reunited, the restoration of social order was imperative. Among other things, this meant that the day world of sober work and the night world of *asobi* (play) had to be separated. In 1589, Hideyoshi authorized the establishment of a licensed pleasure quarter in Kyoto. It was built in Yanagimachi ("Willow Town") near the imperial palace. The district's high-class courtesans drew Kyoto's elite, including Hideyoshi himself. Eventually, the Yanagimachi was to grow into the mighty Shimabara licensed zone. At the same time the *mizujaya*—the early ancestors of Gion's teahouses—were springing up near the Yasaka shrine. Travelers and pilgrims were once more on the move. The long night of war was finally drawing to a close. Hideyoshi died in 1598. Two years later, all Japan was in the hands of the rival Tokugawa family, and they were in power to stay.

An Age of Gold: 1600–1750

The first shogun of the line was Tokugawa Ieyasu, a gray eminence who "used men wisely, shunned the spectacular, and died in bed." [19] He created a rigid society, with a place for everyone and everyone in his place—the word being his, since women were entirely subordinated. Top of the heap were samurai. Next came the farmers, the overworked backbone of society. The artisans followed and finally the merchants. They were despised moneygrubbers. Then there were the underclasses, designated *eta* ("full of filth"), or *hinin* ("non-humans"). These were butchers, tanners, under-

takers, and what the Elizabethans called "sturdy beggars, rogues, vagabonds and actors."

The Tokugawa ideology was Confucianism, revamped for Japanese circumstances. A complete control of society was the only guarantee against a relapse into anarchy. The country was effectively sealed from the outside world. Weapons were confined to the samurai. Laws detailed who could live where, marry who, wear what, and live in what size of house. Romance was not ignored in the new system. "Keep love where it belongs" ran one edict: "in the brothel." Sexual passion had its lowly place, outside the house (*soto*). Marriage was for continuing the family line (*uchi*) and for making alliances. Licensed prostitutes were no threat to society, because they had their place. They were property of the merchant brothel keepers.

Ieyasu chose Edo as the capital of his Orwellian masterpiece. The shogun wanted a city to overshadow Kyoto, which was still the home of the Emperor. The shogun's court became a magnet for all Japan. Right through the 1600s, merchants, samurai, lords, prostitutes, and adventurers piled into this mushrooming boomtown, eager to make their fortunes. The key to Edo's success was that the

Left: Geisha preparing themselves for the evening, while being entertained by a shamisen player. The essential elements of hanamachi life have remained unchanged since the eighteenth century. This watercolor is by Kawahara Keiga (c.1786–1860).

families of all the provincial lords were legally forced to live permanently in the city. The lords themselves had to spend every second year there and their wealth funneled into Edo. Their palaces sprouted up and immediately created vast demand for the luxury goods required to live as a self-respecting "Great Name." This meant that from the beginning, Ieyasu's controlled society was being eaten away from within. The despised merchants were in business and thriving. As their wealth grew, they created a new culture of showy hedonism to rival the excesses of Heian Kyoto.

The first indication that a new popular culture was on the cards came just as Edo was opening for business, in 1603. It was Izumo no Okuni's sensational rise to fame in Kyoto. A dancer and prostitute, she had recognizable *shirabyoshi* roots: she claimed to be an shaman-

istic altar attendant from Shinto's most ancient shrine. But her company's sacred/erotic dance drama, often performed in male drag, was so electrifying that it was immediately recognized as a new art form: kabuki. It gained a nationwide following as the drama of the people, as opposed to the shogunate-sponsored noh. Just like in Restoration London, the actresses were for sale. The government watched with a beady eye. The problem was that, unlike Pepys's London, these companies failed to attract official patronage, though men of all classes paid for these intoxicating players' favors.

In 1629, the government banned women from the stage. Female roles were taken over by adolescent boys. It made no difference. The boys were for sale just as much as the girls had been, and there was no taboo on homosexuality. Kyoto's Miyagawa-cho in particular had reason

Right: The courtesans of the pleasure quarters were perhaps the most fabulously attired group in Japanese history. Samurai as well as merchants were captivated by the Floating World, as this picture demonstrates.

to be grateful, as samurai and Buddhist priests flocked in to enjoy themselves with the boy actors there. By 1652, enough was enough: the kabuki stage was restricted to adult males. Even so, kabuki retained its disreputable image into the twentieth century and it found its natural counterpart in the all-female flower-and-willow world. They remain closely linked, even now when the kabuki world is respectable, pampered, and losing its sense of *iki* by the day.

By the 1660s, the urban merchants were raking in fortunes. Their lives were the polar opposite of the Protestant work ethic. Once they had amassed their gains, they squandered them mainly on sex. Their favored playgrounds were the fabulous Yoshiwara and the Shimabara in Kyoto. These were worlds unto themselves, walled off from the outside, and layed out on reverse feng shui principles. They parodied the Tokugawa social order; the top-level courtesans, *oiran* in Edo and *tayu* in Kyoto, were treated with the etiquette appropriate to provincial lords outside the walls. They refused to sleep with customers they didn't like, and men spent fortunes unsuccessfully courting them.

They were perhaps the most fabulously attired group in Japanese history. Their elaborate coiffures dripped with kilograms of precious metal and tortoiseshell ornaments. Scarlet was the dominant color of their multi-layered robes, with the *obi* tied in front to advertize their sexual availability. Their bare feet were glimpsed under elaborately embroidered over-robes. They wielded enough influence to laugh off the government's

sumptuary laws. Leading courtesans like the legendary Katsuyama were superstars of a hyperactive, commercialized version of the age of Prince Genji. They were the decorated generals of the emerging Floating World. But any slip in the expected standards of costume or deportment could send them tumbling down the ranks.

The foot-soldiers were unfortunate girls sold into the quarters with neither talent nor connections. They sat impassive behind barred windows, as prospective customers wandered by, sizing them up. The Yoshiwara became the setting of countless kabuki plays, a key site in Japanese cultural life. It is of course impossible to quantify the degree of human misery that was suffered between its walls. The girls in their cages burned on more than one occasion in the innumerable fires that swept the city— "the flowers of Edo," as they were called. Their owners, afraid that they might escape, held back from setting them free until it was too late.

For the customers, it was quite different. No shame was attached to visiting the quarters. A night on the tiles was a treasured opportunity for them to escape their regimented lives. The great chronicler of their world is Ihara Saikaku (1642–1693), author of *Five Women Crazy about Love* and *The Life of an Amorous Man*. He was a bon viveur with a natural talent for happiness and a strong resemblance to his contemporary, Samuel Pepys. He was an adept of *senryu*, the satirical brand of haiku popular at the time (for example: *Of all the people in the village / Only the husband does not know.*). He was a world away from his other contemporary Basho, the

No shame was attached to visiting the quarters. A night on the tiles was a treasured opportunity for them to escape their regimented lives.

Right: *The Actor Segawa Kikunojo III as a Courtesan*, by Katsukawa Shun-ei. Kabuki retained a rather disreputable image well into the nineteenth century. The performer's *obi*, with its sash tied at the front, clearly identifies the character as a courtesan.

Things were turning out very differently from Tokugawa Ieyasu's dream of a somber Confucian society. The fun and games were permitted only because they were *asobi* and had no connection with real life outside the walls. Here, the merchants were at the mercy of the shogunate. The more successful of them were regularly stripped of their fortunes by the government, to set an example to any other uppity merchants with ideas above their station. Blowing one's wealth in the Yoshiwara was in fact the sensible course; you might not even get the chance to not take it with you. This cavalier attitude to money became an integral part of the meaning of *iki*.

Taikomochi are products of their time, and they are still the flower-and-willow world's most vocal defenders of extravagant spending.

They ooze contempt at cut-price fun; being cheap is no way for a man to polish his character and it's unspeakably boorish (*buiki*). Arai Shozo is one of the few remaining practitioners of the craft; his customers include men who spend a million Yen at each party. "Spending money in dribs and drabs is no help at all," he advises young businessmen in the current recession. The only way to afford geisha parties is to stop using money in a stingy fashion:

> In today's economic slump, you should
> do things differently from others, other-
> wise you will go down with them…Save
> up for a year and spend all the money in
> one night in a lavish way. That way,
> spending money for fun will come to
> have meaning in your life. [20]

wandering sage who established the form as a serious art. Like his fellow merchants, he regarded the samurai he met in the pleasure districts as boors and bumpkins. He appreciated more the lewd jokes and outrageous dances of the *taikomochi*, who were by now active as male arts practitioners. They played a banjo-like instrument with three strings called the shamisen. It came from the southern island of Okinawa in the late 1500s, and found its route into the *demi-monde* via the *shirabyoshi* dancers.

美人
五面相
人

哥＾麿筆

志くやうふさ～くゑぜく いぢゝあわり
さて目のうち ふ実がうらて 相

Left: *Portrait of a Courtesan Smoking Her Pipe* by Kitagawa Utamaro.

The Birth of the Geisha
1750–1820

For a century after Ihara Saikaku's birth, the scene was dominated by the *tayu* and *oiran* courtesans.

From the government's point of view, walled pleasure quarters at least had the advantage of checkpoints at the gates. The brothel owners reported any suspicious comings and goings. But unlicensed prostitution was on the rise outside the walls, fueled by a growing cash economy. Among the many types of covert prostitutes were the *sancha-joro*, who worked illegally in public bathhouses. The Yoshiwara star Katsuyama started her meteoric career as a humble *sancha-joro*. From the 1680s onward, there were also young women called *odoriko* ("dancing girls"), who were not originally prostitutes as such. Their families had them trained in dance and the other accomplishments, hoping to settle them as concubines in well-off families. As time went by, however, they found themselves having to depend more and more on selling their bodies.

The shogunate's response was unambiguous. Illegal prostitutes were periodically rounded up and thrown into the licensed quarters. In the early 1700s, hundreds of *odoriko* were put into the Yoshiwara. Many came from Fukagawa, the biggest illegal pleasure quarter of them all. They continued to practice their performing arts, even though the law forced them to work as licensed prostitutes. They called themselves *gei-ko* ("arts-child"). This led to the birth of the geisha as a formal profession.

Right: *The Poetess Ono no Komachi* by Harunobu. Ono no Komachi was a renowned ninth-century poet and beauty. Her memory still lives on in the flower-and-willow world.

One of the reasons for the emergence of geisha was that the culture of *tayu* and *oiran* was in steep decline. Standards became lower every time an unfortunate group of prostitutes was press-ganged off the street and into the pleasure quarters. The wealthier customers expected something magical, to spend a night with Ono no Komachi.

What they were increasingly getting for their money was a fling with a bathhouse prostitute. They were dissatisfied, and voted with their wallets. The pleasure quarters reshuffled their ranking system time and again in the mid-eighteenth century, in the desperate hope that promoting sergeants to generals would disguise the fall in sophistication. It didn't work. The list of registered Yoshiwara *oiran* stops blank in 1761. The Yoshiwara remained in business right into the 1950s, a sad shadow of its former self, only frequented by country folk and the urban poor.

Another reason for the changeover to geisha was that most mysterious of transformations: a shift in the sensibility of the age. Clothing and leisure styles toned down in the late eighteenth century. Taste moved from a love of the sumptuous and decorated to an appreciation of the plain and "natural." This change is easier to observe than explain. We can see it in poetry, where a movement of "Back to Basho" writers set out to rescue haiku from the cynical cul-de-sac of the *senryu* style. The trend was the same in *ikebana*, where "global" flower arrangements gave way to the sparser *rikka* ("standing flowers") style. A roughly similar change was underway in Europe at the same time.

The first woman to call herself a geisha was Kiku, from the Fukagawa zone. She announced her new profession in 1750 or 1751. We know nothing about her as an individual, living woman. People of her class were not thought worthy of record, except by the authorities

Left: *Hagoromo (Feather Robe)* by Kimura Buzan. This masterpiece of textile design features a traditional Chinese-derived angelic figure.

environment. Shamisen came from the *taiko-mochi*; dance from the kabuki stage and other traditions stretching right back to the *shirabyoshi*. Her command of the arts was combined with skill in Ogasawara etiquette, but she was its mistress, not its slave. She offered something quite fresh: a chance to enjoy the company of a witty, skilled artistic performer in tastefully refined surroundings. By the eighteenth century, all the elements of geisha arts were in place, including a sophisticated public which was ready to appreciate and patronize the new profession. They included a motley collection of free-spending merchants, rakish young men-about-town, priests out on the tiles, and samurai gone to seed. They were the collective fathers of *tsu*, the lifestyle and aesthetic which was a high-octane mix of men, women, alcohol, high arts, fast money, and cool.

The geisha took off immediately. The new fashion traveled down the Tokaido, the highway linking Edo to the Kyoto-Osaka-Nara heartland of western Japan. They became popular very early in Kyoto, where they appear to have absorbed an emerging female *taikomochi* tradition. Like the *odoriko* in Edo, these performers called themselves geiko, and the name remains used by modern Kyoto geisha. The Yoshiwara drifted along as it was for some years, but 1761 marks the first geisha, as well as the last *oiran* there.

The geisha were so popular that the authorities were powerless to prevent the rise of this new profession. But, like everything else in Japanese life, it still required regulation. The licensed brothel-owners' special concern was

Right: A Japanese hostess, circa 1875. Her *obi* is tied at the back, indicating that she is not engaged in prostitution. While glamorous by comparison, geisha did not look particularly "traditional" until the early twentieth century.

watching the red-light districts. We can infer a good deal about her, however. She was almost certainly from an *odoriko* background, and had worked as a prostitute. Her artistic skills were so developed and in demand that she decided she could make a living from performance alone. She was a star dancer, performer, and shamisen player. She was the direct or indirect heir of all the artistic movements discussed earlier. She was at home performing in a tatami

that the geisha might steal their business. After all, the *odoriko* had started off rather similar to these new-style performers, only to go into competition with the licensed zones almost immediately as prostitutes. Accordingly, the Yoshiwara set up the first *kemban* (geisha registration office) in 1779. The *kemban* system spread nationwide, forming the organizational core of the emerging flower-and-willow world. Geisha were required to attend parties in groups of at least two or three. Their kimono *obi* fastened at the back as a symbol of their non-prostitute status. They were chaperoned by a male companion who carried their shamisen. In theory, they were not allowed to perform after midnight, though the rule was hard to enforce.

By 1820, the flower-and-willow world had taken a form which has remained basically unchanged to this day. In Edo, the geisha performed in *ryotei* restaurants and tearooms called *machiai*. Fukagawa was the early front-runner, with its tough, sassy geisha not a million miles removed from the *odoriko* of old. When walking to their assignments, they insouciantly threw male *haori* jackets over their elegantly understated kimonos, imitating the kabuki female impersonators who were all the rage. Yanagibashi was up and running by this time, and it eventually overtook Fukagawa in the 1830s. In Kyoto they worked the *ochaya* teahouses. In Gion, they were trained in noh-derived dance by teachers of the Inoue School, which had just emerged. Geisha became a licensed profession there in 1813. The all-female *okiya*, or geisha houses, formed as a way of providing the profession with a substitute

Below: A rare triptych by Hiroshige of two geisha on a jetty greeting their colleague, who has arrived by boat to entertain at a party in a restaurant. Another restaurant is shown in the background of the snowy landscape. The umbrella of the geisha in the boat is of the fashionable *janome* type.

family structure. Life outside a family, whether by blood or adoption, was simply unimaginable in Japan at that time.

This support structure was all the more necessary because the economic boom brought on by the long years of peace had run out of steam. The samurai were still paid in rice, and were borrowing hand over fist. They had to do this just to keep up appearances—literally, since sumptuary laws laid down exactly what they had to wear. The countryside was going to rack and ruin. Devastating famines culled the peasantry by the hundreds of thousands. The Tenmei famine of 1782–1787 hit hardest in northern Japan. Entire villages were wiped out. Even townspeople were critically short of food. The government called for restraint in luxury spending and a return to good old morality. The people responded with rice riots and looting.

The general suffering did not affect the urban geisha districts directly. If anything, it helped them get established. With a bit of judicious hoarding, the merchants were able to grow richer off the crisis. Much of their disposable cash went to the old red-light districts or the new geisha quarters. And every time famine visited a locality, a wave of girls and young women washed up in the brothels and hanamachi. They were sold to traders who scoured the land. Selling daughters as a last resort to preserve the family line is an old practice in East Asia, and one of the darkest legacies of Confucianism as a social system.

For all their glamour and artistry, geisha were either born into geisha "families," or sold into them as indentured servants, little better than slaves. However tough their lives were in the hanamachi, they had no legal means of escape unless they paid off their debts to their geisha houses. For the girls from the country, there was usually no question of going back home, even if their homes still existed. The flower-and-willow world was born under these harsh conditions. There is an uncanny resemblance to the period of civil wars and the birth of tea ceremony as a high art. Proud geisha today might be startled at the comparison, but their art form comes from a class of the dispossessed, much as flamenco is the creation of Spanish gypsies, and jazz of African-American slaves.

The other major element of the hanamachi system, *danna* patrons, must also have come into being in the late eighteenth century. Geisha emerged from the world of prostitution as a distinct and separate profession. Indeed, a geisha slogan of the 1870s was "We sell art, not bodies." This was the spirit of the profession, and the *kemban* system was put in place to ensure that the letter of the law was adhered to. Nevertheless, party fees alone were never going to support a geisha. The cost of keeping up the required style was just too exorbitant. The financial gap could not be filled with occasional, casual prostitution as might have been the case for the *odoriko*. The rules of their profession prevented them from marrying. The need was for a dedicated patron to cover the major costs, like a husband but not a husband. In other words, a *danna*, who entered into a formal agreement with the geisha house.

In return for the outlay, the *danna*'s primary gain was in social status. A man who could afford to keep a geisha was visibly successful in business. Since he was seen to be sticking to his end of a very expensive bargain, he was also felt to be a man of his word. His geisha was something like a mistress; she slept with him when he felt the desire. Success in Japan comes with age, however, and most *danna* were getting on in years. Many geisha found themselves not unduly taxed, no doubt to their relief. There was no obligation for a geisha to have just one patron during her career. The geisha-*danna* relationship could last for a lifetime or be as short as six months. In this case, the *danna* paid a substantial severance fee.

A geisha remained free to take lovers if she pleased. As long as she was indentured to a geisha house she was answerable for her time to her Mother, though, and so many affairs were carried on in secret. It was not unknown for money to change hands; then as now, the distinction between what is and is not prostitution sometimes got blurred. In the early days, the Yoshiwara kept the strictest watch on its geisha because it was vital for business to protect the licensed brothels there. Things were much freer in the area of Fukagawa-cho, which was slightly out of town and without a *kemban*.

Evidence of some historic practices in the flower-and-willow world suggest a slightly closer connection to prostitution *per se* than most modern geisha would be comfortable to acknowledge. There were "sleepovers" in the upper rooms of teahouses, for example, where groups of younger geisha would stay the night together with a few high-paying regular guests. Lots of playful grabbing and fumbling went on, but they were not expected to have sex with the guests. However, anecdotal sources report that in the past, some younger geisha were cajoled into spending the night with guests who were not their *danna*. [21] The practice was not regular, or recognized by the *kemban*, but wealthy regular guests could, and did, put a lot of pressure on geisha house Mothers to get sexual access to young geisha.

In any case, the *danna* was expected to turn a blind eye; being jealous in public would be the height of bad form. It would also be an open confession that the *danna* was mean and/or could not keep "his woman" in line.

Left: *Hana-Ogi of Ogi-Ya* by Utamaro.

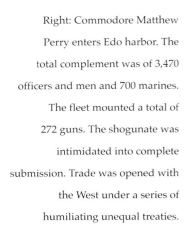

Right: Commodore Matthew Perry enters Edo harbor. The total complement was of 3,470 officers and men and 700 marines. The fleet mounted a total of 272 guns. The shogunate was intimidated into complete submission. Trade was opened with the West under a series of humiliating unequal treaties.

And, the thinking went, if a man can't even keep a woman in line, how can he be trusted with the serious things in life, like business, money, and the rigors of honorable conduct?

The deflowering of the apprentice geisha by the *mizuage danna* when she was fifteen or even younger was a separate and open practice. In Kyoto, the apprentice geisha's hairstyle was changed to the *ofuku* arrangement, to publicly signify that she was now an adult woman. The *mizuage danna* were local notable businessmen with close ties to the hanamachi. There was no permanent bond between the two parties; the connection ended as soon as the girl's ordeal was over.

The sad fact is that enforced sex with a stranger at the age of fifteen or so was the norm for Japanese women in most walks of life. Girls were married off young, with little or no heed paid to their personal inclinations. Though their lives were often hard, the geisha at least had the opportunity to sample a little freedom, variety, and fun. The most successful of them were stars, in demand by the movers and shakers of the age. They were sought after by heartthrobs of the kabuki stage, and lionized in *ukiyo-e* woodblock prints, which reached their height of development just as the geisha profession took shape. We have come across the word *ukiyo* before, in the Warring States period, when it referred to the miserable transience of life in a war-torn world. From the age of Ihara Saikaku it changed meaning. Now, it expressed a fascination at the fabulous lightness of being in the play-world of the licensed quarters.

Because *ukiyo-e* prints were cheap and mass-marketed, they are a good barometer of people's concerns. Kabuki stars, *tayu*, *oiran*, and later, geisha beauties by artists like Kitagawa Utamaro (1753–1806) were the stock in trade. People yearned for beauty, if only on paper. The landscapes and travelogues of Hokusai (1760–1849) and Hiroshige (1797–1858) tell another story. Travel in Tokugawa Japan required internal passports and most people were hemmed into their local lordships. They could only experience traveling the Tokaido highway through *ukiyo-e*, and they must have longed for broader horizons. The popularity of Hokusai and Hiroshige tells us that they did.

Travel was restricted. Political discussion was banned outright. Information from the outside world trickled through in dribs and drabs through the Dutch traders at Dejima island in Nagasaki. The first generations of

geisha lived out their lives, happy or unhappy as chance dictated. But the society they lived in was slowly rotting away from within.

The Apogee of the Geisha 1820–1870

The situation became more critical as the Western colonial powers started to approach. The Portuguese and Spanish had been seen off in the 1600s and the Dutch were confined to Nagasaki harbor. Now the foreigners were back, with an intimidating range of modern weaponry. The Russians were dangerously close to Hokkaido, and the British were pushing for more trading rights in East Asia. The tide of the times was made brutally clear by

Left: Okichi of Shimoda, mistress of Townsend Harris, and a tragic national heroine in Japan. An American ship departs on the horizon. In 1945, women were hastily recruited to serve as prostitutes to the arriving Allied occupiers. They were officially urged to defend Japanese womanhood, as "the Okichis of the present era."

Right: The opening of Japan led to a wave of photographers visiting the country. This photograph dates from circa 1865.

natural right of men of a certain status. Even the Dutch traders in Nagasaki had been provided with licensed prostitutes by the state. For an accredited diplomat, however, this clearly would not do. Attention turned to two young Shimoda geisha, Okichi and Ofuku. Okichi, destined for Harris's bed, was horrified when approached. To become known as a foreigner's concubine would ruin her for life. But the Shimoda authorities cajoled and coerced her; eventually the two girls went to the mission. The legend of *Madame Butterfly* was born.

Britain's victory over China in the Opium War of 1839–1842. The continental titan, with its revered and ancient culture, was humbled by a sea-borne wave of drug pushers. Japan was clearly next in line.

In 1853, it happened: six black warships of the United States East India Squadron sailed into Edo bay. The shogunate was powerless to stop them. Their commander, Commodore Matthew Perry, demanded a peace treaty and free trade. It was signed and was quickly followed by treaties with Britain, Russia, and the Netherlands. Tokugawa Ieyasu's intricate mechanism of state was now openly falling to pieces.

Townsend Harris arrived in Japan as America's first consul general in 1856, and settled in Shimoda, about a hundred miles southwest of Edo. This rotund fifty-two year-old gentleman immediately caused a knotty protocol problem: he was single despite his years and requested companions for himself and his young Dutch assistant. The authorities were not particularly troubled by the request itself. It was felt that access to women was a

The relationship between Okichi and Harris was brief and, by all accounts, unhappy. Harris eventually moved to Edo in 1857, and took up with another, presumably coerced, woman there. Okichi was abandoned and ruined. No man would become the patron of a foreigner's ex-concubine. The decade or so of her remaining life was dark, lonely, and drink-sodden. She is sentimentally remembered as a sacrificial victim on the altar of Japan-US relations. It took over a century for the first Japanese feminist critics to point out that the ones who sacrificed her were the good burghers of Shimoda. Male Japan lamented its "sacrifice," suffered none of the pain and continued to allow hundreds of girls to be sold into prostitution yearly.

The Hollywood version of the story is equally sentimental. John Huston's 1958 *The Barbarian and the Geisha*, starring John Wayne and Eiko Ando, features a full-blown romance between the star-crossed couple. Fighting her way through a storm of celluloid cliches, Okichi foils an assassination attempt on Harris, etc. In Japan's Okichi myth, Japan plays the stoic sufferer; in the American version, America is the universally beloved.

The samurai class would have doubtless begged to differ. The popular slogan among them at this time was *sonno joi*—revere the emperor and expel the barbarians. This thinking was particularly strong in two feudal domains, Choshu at the western tip of Honshu, and Satsuma in southwestern Kyushu. Satsuma was a very distinctive fief, a Japanese Sparta with a huge and exceptionally macho samurai population. Many of them took to the road, in search of like-minded radicals from elsewhere in Japan. They naturally gravitated to Kyoto, home of the imperial court. Once in the city, they beat an equally natural path to the *ochaya*. Where better to plot than in a meeting place where the staff had a rigid code of secrecy? And were pretty to boot? The flower-and-willow world, especially Gion Kobu, became closely and often romantically involved with the dashing young pro-imperial radicals. These men included a constellation of talent. Among many others from Choshu were Ito Hirobumi and Yamagata Aritomo and, from Satsuma, Matsutaka Masayoshi and Kuroda Kiyotaka—all of them future prime ministers. We can see something of their caliber in Matsutaka's remark, urging his fellow-conspirators to use all the money at their disposal:

> If we do not succeed in overthrowing the Tokugawa government, we will all die together but, if we win, there is no limit to what we will all have. [22]

Not all of these men spent time in Kyoto, but the leisure culture of the fledgling ruling class received an indelible tint of the Kyoto hanamachi. For many aficionados of the flower-and-willow world, this was indeed its finest hour.

The Choshu-Satsuma alliance was cemented in 1866, opening the way for the definitive *coup d'etat*. The shogunate had proved itself inept politically, and it fared no better on the battlefield. In 1868, the regime folded. The fifteen-year-old Emperor Meiji was borne in triumph to Edo, to be restored. Power in fact passed to the young samurai of Satsuma and Choshu. They paraded the coup as the Meiji Restoration. In fact, they were about to embark on the greatest social revolution ever seen in Asia.

Left: Poster for *The Geisha*, Daly's Theatre, London, 1896. As well as epitomising nineteenth-century *Japonisme*, this poster is one of the earliest examples of the word "geisha" in print in English.

The Rebirth of the Geisha, 1868–1958

The Meiji Period (1868–1912)

Japan was a nation being reborn, and the early decades of the Meiji period were a crazy patchwork of bowler hats and men's kimonos. Japanese society was forcibly shoved into the modern world. Kishii Yoshie's compendious *Onna geisha no jidai* ("The Age of the Female Geisha") lists the following events for 1871: beef and handkerchiefs popular (July); freedom of travel proclaimed (July); marriages between nobles and commoners permitted; caps become popular for the first time (August). [23]

The flower-and-willow world was reborn in two different ways. The Tokyo hanamachi were given an enormous shot in the arm by the arrival of the new governing class, many of them fresh from Gion. Large numbers of highly skilled geisha accompanied them. The new state was a much friendlier environment. The Tokugawa class system was abolished; geisha were no longer legally less than samurai. Indeed, girls of samurai origin were soon forming as much as a third of new apprentice intakes. It was the same old story; their families had picked the losing side in the Meiji-Tokugawa struggle. The geisha's all-male mirror society, kabuki, rose in status, too. Noh drama lost its state backing. The Meiji emperor even attended a kabuki play in 1887. The Akasaka geisha district (near what is now the Diet building) had formed by 1873. There were complaints that many of the women working there were not *bona fide* geisha, however. There

were now 635 licensed geisha in Tokyo. [24] This number mushroomed in the 1880s with the growth of government and business.

Geisha were now confidantes to the power-brokers, and not a few married prominent politicians. This would have been unthinkable under the shogunate. Ito Hirobumi, Japan's first prime minister, was a dedicated and highly energetic patron of Tokyo's geisha quarters. A short poem of his vividly captures the new elite's mindset of work and play:

> Asleep with one's head in the lap of a
>   beauty,
> One awakens at dawn
> To resume the mantle of empire [25]

Things were very different in Kyoto. The departure of the emperor was a massive blow to the city's self-esteem. Even now, it is a bitter memory. In the early 1870s, it was a crisis. To cope, the city started on a very modern exercise indeed: rebranding. Kyoto was now to market itself as the center of all things traditional. This was an age of great international exhibitions, and Kyoto got in on the act in 1871. The flower-and-willow world was an obvious resource for drawing business, and the annual Cherry Dances were established the next year. The program was put together by the governor of Kyoto, the ninth-generation head of the Ichiriki *ochaya*, and the third-generation head of the Inoue School of dance. This was quite a radical departure for the geiko and maiko. They had never before performed in public for all comers. They had never before been asked to symbolize anything, let alone Japanese tradition.

Japan was a nation being reborn.

Left: Ito Hirobumi (1831–1909), a former samurai from Choshu and first prime minister of Japan. His grandee's uniform, encrusted with medals, clearly illustrates the new regime's desire to westernize the country. He was also a noted bon vivant and womanizer.

Right: Foreigners began to settle in Japan as technicians and advisers in the 1860s. Their strange appearance and habits fascinated the Japanese. Artists like Hiroshige III used them as exotic details. Here two foreigners ride horses near Mount Fuji. Telegraph wires, a newly introduced invention, stretch across the countryside.

Far right: A girl dressed in a floral patterned kimono, photographed circa 1895. The international image of Japan became steadily feminized and eroticized after the Meiji Restoration. This was largely a result of Western interest in geisha.

Thankfully, it was all a splendid success. The people of Kyoto took the annual event to their hearts, and it became a treasured event in their elaborate calendar. Old-timers fondly recall its mix of high sophistication and familiar good humor, which melted away in later years as the audience became packed with out-of-towners and even foreigners.

The other new development in Kyoto was the formation of the Gion Kobu Professional Female Training Company, or Kabukai, a controlling body of the hanamachi and its school, the Yasaka Nyokoba Academy. The Kyoto flower-and-willow world was forced to evolve to survive, and it was organizationally ahead of Tokyo until the turn of the century.

The Japanese state was still very shaky, with its trade and tariffs in foreign control, and there were real fears that it might not be fully recognized by the West. In 1872, an incident happened which helped put those worries to rest, and impinged directly on the flower-and-willow world. The *Maria Luz*, a Peruvian-registered ship damaged at sea, docked in Yokohama harbor. A fugitive swam to the shore. He was a slave from China, one of over two hundred on board. Here was a golden opportunity for Japan to prove itself a modern state in the eyes of the world. The government seized the ship, arrested the captain, and freed the slaves. Slavery had no legal basis in the modern world, proclaimed the Japanese prosecutors. Slavery had a definite place in Japan, replied the Peruvian defendants, in the Yoshiwara and every other licensed district which accepted women for sale.

The government won the case and it was a crucial victory proving that Japan was a member of the community of nations on the basis of international law. But the Peruvian defence argument had embarrassed the government so much that it immediately set about legal reform of the licensed districts and the hanamachi. Before the year was out, it had passed the Prostitute and Geisha Emancipation Act. It was also known as the Cattle Release Act, because it characterized the plight of these women as akin to farm animals being expected to pay off debts.

For a while, it looked as though the red-light districts and geisha quarters would empty. The Yoshiwara was dark for weeks. But it gradually became apparent that many of the "emancipated" women had nowhere else to go. The red-light districts resumed business under new names and girls continued to join the hanamachi, not sold but "adopted"—for a fee. The Emancipation Act had positive results for the flower-and-willow world: it reemphasized the legal distinction between geisha and prostitutes. It also encouraged the creation of training schools for working women. In the Kyoto hanamachi, these quickly evolved into geisha training schools like the Yasaka Nyokoba Academy.

There were now over six hundred geisha in Tokyo. Yanagibashi, with its river and pleasure boats, was now the undisputed mistress of the hanamachi. Its nearest rivals were the newer Shimbashi and Akasaka districts. Fukagawa had long since fallen by the wayside, lost to a police crackdown on its free-and-easy geisha in 1843. The hanamachi system continued to become more firmly defined: fee scales for geisha parties were formally set for the first time in 1874. By 1878, the Tokyo hanamachi even had their own trade paper, the *Iroha Shimbun* (ABC Newspaper). The flower-and-willow world there finally took definitive shape in 1895. A deal brokered between the powers-that-be in Yanagibashi and Shimbashi consolidated the Tokyo geisha districts into compact, set areas, and formed the nucleus of the All-Japan Union of Geisha Houses. This body had no separate offices or staff. It worked as a mediating agency, with five or fewer representatives in each hanamachi, regulating geisha business conduct along with the local *kemban*. Only the Yoshiwara stayed aloof , and regional membership outside Tokyo increased steadily. [26]

The craze for all things Western reached its height during the 1880s. Its most tangible

Right: A poster for *The Mikado*, which opened in London in March 1885. The *Japonisme* boom lasted into the next century, peaking again with Sadayakko's tours of the West in 1900–1902. The musical also enjoyed considerable success on the Japanese stage.

symbol was the Rokumeikan, or Pavilion of the Deer Cry, an overblown Western-style wedding cake of a building which served as a dancehall and restaurant to Tokyo's elite. Dance practice was held every Monday from nine to four, with Japanese ladies in hoops on the arms of the foreign experts in engineering and economics who had been hired by the government in droves. Of course, many of the ladies learning to waltz were geisha. Dinner at the Rokumeikan cost 20 Yen. A mid-level bureaucrat earned 50 Yen a month. The climax of the revels was reached in 1888, with a grand fancy dress ball which the leading lights of the government attended, dressed up as knights, minstrels, and jesters. A reaction naturally set in against these excesses and taste swung back to Japanese fashions. By the next year, only middle-ranking bureaucrats were wearing Western dress at the Rokumeikan.

Nevertheless, these were the years when the traditional geisha look and average women's fashions started to part company. Until then, the flower-and-willow world had been a more gorgeous version of its drabber everyday sister. "Japanese ladies' hairstyles" thundered the Ladies' Association "are unhealthy, uneconomical, inconvenient and to be got rid of immediately." Even standards of physical beauty were changing. Before, the required look had included a round face, with almond-shaped eyes delicately tilted up at the corners; now, taller girls with prominent noses were in vogue. They suited Western clothes better. [27] In fact, it was only now, as society westernized rapidly, that geisha started to become noticeably "tradi-

tional" in their looks and entertainment. This was a slow process, which lasted into the period after 1945.

Japan was fascinated by the West; the reverse was also true. A wave of Japanese fashion swept Europe in the late nineteenth century, most notably in the visual arts. The contribution of the geisha community was, naturally, mainly in the areas of theater, dance, and music. A good example of the dynamic of *Japonisme* in action is the following picture of the rehearsals for Gilbert and Sullivan's *The Mikado*, which opened at London's Savoy Theatre on March 14, 1885:

> Just at that time a company of Japanese had arrived in England and set up a little village of their own in Knightsbridge. Society hastened to be Japanned, just as a few years ago Society had been aestheti-cised. Through the courtesy of the directors of the Knightsbridge Village, a Japanese male dancer and a Japanese tea-girl were permitted to give their services to the Savoy management.
>
> The Geisha, or Tea-girl, was a charming and very able instructress, although she knew only two words of English – "Sixpence, please," that being the price of a cup of tea as served by her at Knightsbridge. To her was committed the task of teaching our ladies Japanese deportment, how to walk or run or dance in tiny steps with toes turned in, as gracefully as possible; how to spread

A wave of Japanese fashion swept Europe in the late nineteenth century, most notably in the visual arts.

and snap the fan either in wrath, delight, or homage and how to giggle behind it.[28]

Over three dozen Japanese theater troupes toured the West during the Meiji period. The most successful by far was the Imperial Japanese Theatre Company, led by the kabuki actor Kawakami Otojiro and his wife, the celebrated ex-geisha Sadayakko. She was from Tokyo's Nihombashi district and at the top of her profession: her patron was Ito Hirobumi, four times the prime minister. She eventually married Kawakami, an ambitious actor-impresario who realized that huge demand existed for Japanese performers in the West, especially with a glamorous female heroine. Their tours through America and Europe from 1900 to 1902 were a sensation. Gide, Debusy, and Rodin saw their kabuki spectaculars at the Paris Exposition of 1900. The young Picasso sketched the exotic geisha dancing wildly. Puccini saw them in Milan in 1902 and their music had a direct influence on *Madame Butterfly*, which he composed the next year. Sadayakko survived all the way to 1946; she was seventy-four.

The other geisha of international repute during these years was Oyuki, a Gion beauty who married the fabulously wealthy American George Dennison Morgan, nephew of the banker J. Pierpont Morgan. The fortune he spent in pursuit of her was so vast that the Japanese dailies followed his expenditure with bated breath. A musical was written based on the courtship. The couple eventually settled in Paris, where Morgan died suddenly, aged forty-four. Oyuki Morgan returned to Kyoto in 1938, the most celebrated ex-geisha of her generation.

Oyuki and Morgan married in 1904. Japan was preparing to stun the world with its military prowess in the Russo-Japanese war. It fought titanic battles in Manchuria, and put the Russian Baltic fleet to the bottom of the Korea Strait. The flower-and-willow world displayed intense patriotism, just as it had in the war against China ten years earlier. The Tokyo hanamachi feted troops passing through the city to the front. When the victory was won the next year, the capital erupted. So many parties were held that numerous new geisha entertainment rooms and geisha houses were founded in 1905. Yanagibashi introduced a new public dance performance to celebrate Japan's military glory. The entertainment rooms or *machiai* became rather notorious, prompting stiffer regulations the same year from the All-Japan Union of Geisha Houses: no fully-qualified geisha under twenty, no double-jobbing, and all geisha to be officially registered with geisha houses.

The jubilation was short-lived in any case. The Treaty of Portsmouth, which ended the Russo-Japanese war, confirmed Japan's gains in Korea and Manchuria, but denied her the indemnities most people expected as a right. Nationalist protestors took to the streets; martial law was declared in Tokyo. A particular target of the mob's wrath was Okoi ("Honorable Carp"), an ex-geisha and long-time mistress to the serving prime minister, Katsura Taro of Choshu. Like a Japanese Nell Gwyn, she was rounded on hysterically for the failings of her powerful lover. Okoi was the most flamboyant

Japan's expanding power brought some exotic new faces to the hanamachi.

Left: Geisha in the 1920s. This is the time setting of the Arthur Golden novel *Memoirs of a Geisha*. The girls photographed here seem little more than children. Many thousands like them were effectively sold into the hanamachi.

geisha, eighteen and nineteen years old, arrived from the newly-occupied territory of Hokkaido. Called Pajuro and Gujuro, they astonished the capital with their appetites for food. They apparently worked through two sacks of sweet potatoes in the first four days after their arrival, while calling for rice at the same time. [29]

The hanamachi were cast into darkness once more during the final illness of the Meiji emperor in 1912. Both Japan and the flower-and-willow world had changed beyond recognition since his accession. Both were richer, more powerful, and more respected internationally than they could have dreamed back in 1868, when the angry samurai first seized power.

The Taisho Period (1912–1926)

The reign of the new emperor Taisho started out in a mood of optimism. The heavy hands of the authoritarian elder statesmen were weakening. It seemed that the time for the Diet to rule had finally come. A popular song of the time was *Demokurashii Bushi* ("the Song of Democracy"). Yet another Tokyo hanamachi opened in 1913. Lesbianism, records Kishii, was the "in" thing in March that year. World War I was bloodless and very profitable for Japan and all to the good of the flower-and-willow world. Shimbashi hosted the adored Charlie Chaplin on a goodwill visit in 1915. *Ginbura*—strolling the Ginza in Tokyo—was in fashion. A popular and free-spirited *boulevardier* culture was on the rise. Before entering a convent, the ex-geisha Okoi opened a shop on the Ginza. In keeping with the times, it was not a teashop but a bar. By war's end, the avenue was packed with

of geisha, a product of the Shimbashi district. Her affairs covered the spectrum of high society, from kabuki actors to sumo wrestlers, from financiers to the prime minister himself. She survived the riots of 1905 and spent the final phase of her life as a Buddhist nun.

Japan's expanding power brought some exotic new faces to the Tokyo hanamachi. Three Taiwanese geisha are recorded in Nihonbashi in 1908. Two years later, a pair of young Ainu

restaurants, bars, and cafés, showing all the signs of Weimar Germany's decadence with none its defeatism.

The main difference between European and Japanese cafés of the time was that the waitresses in Japan were paid no wages whatsoever and relied entirely on the customers. Café culture was in fact based on prostitution. The Ginza of the Roaring Twenties was often quite over the top. One example was the "Organ Service," a bizarre precursor of the excesses of the 1980s:

> The waitress, usually not wearing underwear, sat in a booth on the laps of a number of customers. The customers touched her wherever they felt like, and she emitted a sound ranging from bass to soprano depending. Carnal transactions were not uncommonly carried out there. [30]

If biblical-style wrath seemed called for, it hit Tokyo on September 1, 1923, in the form of the Great Kanto Earthquake. It leveled the city, killing almost a hundred thousand. Thousands more were lost in the hysterical bloodletting which followed, directed against the resident Korean community and largely unhindered by the police.

The hanamachi suffered little enough. In fact, the boom years of the twenties were a golden age, and two new districts opened in Tokyo. The *taikomochi* Yugentei Tamasuke's memoirs record a free and earthy social scene, with the magical waterside Yanagimachi at its apex. The collapse of Czarist Russia brought yet more foreign faces into the flower-and-willow world. 1920 saw three Russian geisha debut in Akasaka, as well as, ironically, Japan's first Mayday celebrations. Yugentei recalls working

Left: A trio of senior geisha wearing formal black crested kimonos.

with a White Russian *taikomochi*, as well as a female *taikomochi* called Virginia. [31]

For all its vulgarity and prejudice, there was a sense of openness in Japan rarely rivaled before or since. It was felt in the hanamachi and in the outside world, too. The workers were no longer corporate samurai. They hopped from job to job as opportunity directed. The main artistic development of the period for geisha was the first staging of the public Azuma Odori dances in Shimbashi during the year of 1926.

The shadows were starting to lengthen, however. Japanese politics were already highly authoritarian. The military had cornered a permanent seat in the cabinet at the turn of the century. A draconian Peace Preservation Law was passed in 1925, drastically cutting down on political freedoms. Japan was about to enter its second age of iron.

The Early Showa Period (1926–1945)
The Great Depression changed the tone very quickly. In Japan as in Germany, economic

Below: In a pose which would not look out of place in an Utamaro woodblock print, a geisha holds a pen in her mouth after writing on a long roll of paper. The photograph dates from 1906.

dislocation gave fascism its chance. By the mid-thirties, appalled reporters were filing stories from the north of Japan telling of children on the brink of starvation. Their lives were not significantly different from the famine-stricken peasants of the late eighteenth century. Waves of young girls were once more being sold, not just into the brothels and geisha districts of Japan but as far afield as Hong Kong and Singapore. Their brothers were in the army, and spoiling for radical change.

Rafts of oppressive legislation were brought in. The state was lauded and emperor worship became its official cult. The army increasingly ran amok in China, with the government unwilling or unable to stop it. The authorities turned prim, hectoring, and hypocritical. In 1931, the police ordered separated seating for men and women in movie halls. One wonders what Ihara Saikaku, Pepy's contemporary, would have thought if he'd wandered in for a look. Which would have puzzled him more—the moving pictures or the segregated seating? It was all most unJapanese. This was a country which banned mixed bathhouses only because Victorian tourists had protested for their own, inscrutable reasons. The police had banned the first ever stage production of *The Tale of Genji* in 1933. It was too decadent.

The Ministry of Education was an enthusiastic tout of fascist thinking. In 1937, it published the tract *Kokutai no hongi* ("The Fundamentals of the National Polity"), attacking democracy and individualism, and calling on the people to "abandon one's small ego" and "live for the great glory and dignity of the

emperor." [32] The geisha world kept its head down carefully. Doubtless some of them heard their military clients muttering rumors about the army's slaughter of over 200,000 civilians at Nanking that year.

They did have one notable success, however—a boycott of the mighty Toho media empire in 1935. A Toho-owned magazine had printed a scathing article on slipping standards in the

Above: The caption of this photo, from 1931, reads: "Dr. Bascom Johnson of the U.S. seated at the right, with members of the League of Nations White Slave Commission, during a visit to the geisha quarter of Tokyo." Japan renounced League membership two years later.

Right: Geisha, wearing aprons over their kimonos, serving Japanese sailors on Tokyo Navy Day, 1937. The sashes slung across their backs identify them as members of the *Dai Nippon kokubo fujin kai*, or Ladies' Defense League of Greater Japan. Japanese society was extensively militarized during the 1930s. A stream of rationed goods flowed into the hanamachi from military patrons.

flower-and-willow world. The geisha organizations were not amused and exercised their muscle both publically through boycott and privately through leaning on their well-connected clients. The row was sorted out later that year in a deal brokered by the police. Toho did not bother the flower-and-willow world again.

Controls tightened as the nation slid into total war. Neon, longhaired students, and perms for women were banned in 1939. Restaurants were closed early and kept totally closed every month on "Co-prosperity Day." Rationing was introduced the next year. Dance halls were shut down. Cigarette brands with English names like "Bat" and "Cherry" were changed into Japanese. The government started a "Luxury is the Enemy" campaign. Luckily, the authorities were completely hypocritical and continued to patronize the geisha districts. The military in particular ensured a steady underground stream of rationed goods.

There was a Communist underground in Japan, but the most popular expression of dissent was a retreat into apathy or a frantic chase after pleasure. Jazz was popular, with hits like *Shanghai Flowergirl* and *Rainy Blues*. As in Germany, jazz was banned during the war. The police preferred melodies like *Father, You Were Strong* and *Heroes of the Air*.

By the end of 1941, Japan was at war with every major world power except Germany and Russia. At home, the war started to bite very quickly. By 1943 most unmarried women under twenty-six were being inducted into national service. Gion Kobu Kaburenjo (geisha theater) was turned into a munitions factory. The flower-and-willow world was now under direct threat. The war situation was so serious that even its awe-inspiring network of contacts could not save it. Even Gion Kobu's donation of two fighter planes to the military was of no avail. The geisha scrambled to find safe jobs and avoid being drafted into the factories, where undernourished children worked hellish eighteen-hour days. Some were in time, while others were not. On March 5, 1944, the flower-and-willow world was disbanded by government order.

The Pacific island of Saipan came under American control, putting Tokyo and other major cities within bombing range. The single biggest raid came on March 9, 1945, when 334 B-29s firebombed central Tokyo. It was a visitation of hell upon the earth. Canals boiled. Ninety-seven thousand died in the firestorm, which obliterated the Tokyo hanamachi. [33] Many other cities fared equally badly, but Kyoto was spared. Legend has it that the curator of the Smithsonian pleaded with Roosevelt to save it. Nevertheless, large areas of the city were pulled down to form firebreaks in case of bombing. The beautiful riverside Ponto-cho district suffered worst. There were geisha too, in Hiroshima and Nagasaki. On August 15, at twelve noon, the emperor addressed the people, instructing them the "endure the unendurable" and lay down their arms.

Left: A corpse lays in the ruins of Nanking station after a Japanese air raid during the Sino-Japanese conflict, 1937. With their advanced network of military contacts, geisha would have been among the first Japanese civilians to learn of the massacre. Their code of conduct, however, forbade them to divulge such information. "The Rape of Nanjing" is regularly denied to this day in Japan.

Mid-Showa 1945–1959

The shattered flower-and-willow world began to pull itself back into being in 1946 and 1947. Geisha returned from the countryside, riding packed trains into the ruined and starving cities. Their clientele was different from before. After the war ended and before the American occupation began, the Japanese elite looted vast stocks of army surplus material. Most of it ended up in the black market. Corrupt officials and black market bosses were a major source of custom for the geisha. These were truly desperate years for most people. Tens of thousands of women found themselves working as *pan-pan*, or street prostitutes. They were so common that "playing *pan-pan*" became a popular children's game. Another source of hanamachi clientele was, of course, the officer class of the US army of occupation. The middle-ranking officers seem to have been particularly common visitors, though it is doubtful that many had any understanding of the language or culture. Many prostitutes passed themselves off as geisha to the Americans, who neither knew nor cared.

As we saw before in the story of Townsend Harris and Okichi, the Japanese authorities felt that sex was one of the rights of powerful men. They also feared that the Americans would engage in mass rape. They therefore organized brothels for the occupying army, staffed by over a thousand women of the Recreation and Amusement Association. The women they were assembling, they declared, would be "the Okichis of the present era." [34]

One bright aspect of these years was that democratic politics finally arrived in Japan,

The women they were assembling, they declared, would be "the Okichis of the present era."

albeit at the point of an American gun. The new constitution, written in English by the occupation forces, guaranteed gender equality and gave women the franchise for the first time. Many successfully stood for election. The old family system was now seen as belonging to the imperialistic past. In the new Japan, women were to have the right to decide their own lives, including whether to marry, and who. Against this background, mass prostitution seemed an

even more glaring anomaly. The RAA was wound down by MacArthur in 1946, and a strong civic movement to ban licensed prostitution developed soon after the war. The idea was strongly resisted by everyone with a commercial interest, and the debate dragged on for years. The law finally came into effect in 1959.

It marked the end of an era for geisha as well as prostitutes. The two separate worlds had lived side by side for centuries, one a mirror image of the other. Now the Yoshiwara closed its doors. *Mizuage* or ceremonial deflowering became a thing of the past. *Danna* patronage was now prohibited, officially at least. And the forced adoption of children into the hanamachi ceased. The geisha had made yet another transformation—into a freely-chosen profession, in a much freer society. The only question was how to survive in this unexpected, brave new world.

Left: A group of geisha, 1937. The social upheavals of the 1930s changed the flower-and-willow world relatively little. Real changes and traumatic experiences lay in wait for these women during the following decade.

CHAPTER 3

becoming a geisha

The flagship of the whole geisha enterprise in Japan is the maiko.

Right: A maiko in Kyoto. Her hairstyle indicates that she is still relatively new to the profession.

Far right: The maiko look exerts an enduring fascination in Japan even today.

We must labour to be beautiful

William Butler Yeats, *Adam's Curse*

In this section on recruitment and training, we concentrate mainly on the scene in Kyoto. The flagship of the whole geisha enterprise in Japan is the maiko—that is, the trainee geisha who is unique to the city of Kyoto alone. In fact when most Westerners hear the word "geisha," the picture that flashes into their minds will be based, in however distorted a fashion, on the white make-up and sumptuous hair ornaments of the maiko. No other city better preserves the fantastic complexity of rank and the rigors of Ogasawara etiquette at its strictest.

Recruitment

In the dismal past, many girls became geisha through no wish of their own. Their families could not afford to keep them and thought that the flower-and-willow world was at least better than the alternatives. Sometimes age was a factor. Trainee geisha traditionally started their careers aged just six years, six months, and six days. In contrast to the West, the number combination was auspicious, especially for new beginnings.

Nowadays, girls and young women enter the flower-and-willow world for all sorts of reasons. One, of course, is being born into it. The birth of female children has always been welcomed in the hanamachi precisely because they can become geisha, with none of the strains of adopting an outsider into the family involved. Other people may have looser family connections, or come from a related craft background, like kimono design. However, these days it is quite normal for new recruits to arrive from perfectly humdrum middle-class families, simply because they are in love with the gorgeous

Right: These performers are bound for the 250-year-old *Kamezaki* ("Scent of Plum Blossoms") restaurant in Sakata.

geisha look, and want to give the lifestyle a try. Some are even hoping to walk down the aisle with a movie star or sportsman.

But the arrival of a new hopeful from regular "civilian" life is not very common—at least, not common enough to keep the flower-and-willow world from slowly but ominously shrinking. To join the flower-and-willow world involves overcoming some formidable psychological barriers. The first is parental disapproval. Geisha has never made it into the top ten list of careers parents long for their daughters to follow. Many Japanese people still, and mistakenly, mix up geisha with the courtesans of old. Also, the parents are often a lot more clued-in about just how rigorous the training and etiquette will be. After all, they themselves were brought up by the previous, stricter generation.

A second barrier is that the young aspirant will have to sever links with her natural family almost completely. Here, she will be under no illusions, whatever her age. In all serious Japanese traditional arts, the novice "walks the talk." From sword-making to *rakugo* story-telling, Japanese apprentices learn by watching someone who really knows what they're doing. That means living under the same roof as your teacher.

There are other considerations. The Ministry of Education does not recognize the arts training offered at the geisha schools. Sumo prodigies go through college on sports scholarships; trainee geisha may not even get a high school diploma. What happens, the parents wonder, if their daughter drops out of training?

The dilemmas are familiar to families in the West with talented (or wishful) young basketball or soccer players. The parents will also be uneasily aware of the huge debts she will build up during training, which she will have to pay back to her *okiya* (geisha house.)

Above: A lady dressed up as a historical *tayu* (Kyoto courtesan), probably for a festival. The *tayu* tradition continues to be re-enacted in the Shimabara district of Kyoto.

Nobody *needs* to become a geisha in today's Japan. Increasingly few do. Attracting new trainees has become so difficult that, a few years ago, two Kyoto hanamachi actually resorted to putting advertisements in magazines. It was a sign of growing desperation. One simply doesn't do this kind of thing in the flower-and-willow world, where face-to-face connections are the basic rule. The tactic was quickly and shamefacedly abandoned.

There are, of course, fashions within the Kyoto geisha districts, too. Gion Kobu may be the most prestigious of them all, but many of the young women entering the hanamachi these days feel more at ease with Miyagawa-cho's more relaxed ambience. Artistic standards are of course high, but the etiquette doesn't feel quite as starchy. So this hanamachi gets more than its fair share of precious recruits, leaving that many fewer for the others.

Her real job is to acclimatize herself to the rhythms of hanamachi life.

Shikomi

Once she has moved into the *okiya* (geisha house), the apprentice starts off on the lowest rung. Her schedule is set, rigid, and exhausting. She is called a *shikomi*, and her job, in the formal sense, is essentially to scrub floors, look tidy, and learn the rudiments of dance, shamisen, percussion, and flute. She also may have to finish school (people graduate junior high school at about fifteen). Her real job is to acclimatize herself to the rhythms of hanamachi life. She also has to get used to living in a traditional tatami environment, and wearing traditional clothes—nothing fancy, just simple

striped kimonos and light *yukata* robes. Above all, she has to forge relationships with her house Mother, the geiko (Kyoto geisha), perhaps a maiko also, and other staff. She is expected to be *genki*—cheerful and with a have-a-go attitude—and to be appropriately polite, especially in the set greetings that form such an important part of traditional everyday life.

It can be very tough. Especially if she comes from a typical modern Japanese family, the *okiya* lifestyle comes as an often unexpected culture shock. After all, this is Japan, her own country. Her parental home has one tatami mat room, used for special occasions, and she may have worn kimonos before, also on special occasions like weddings and so forth. But it is all relentlessly different. Every room is a tatami room. All the clothes are traditional. Even the Japanese language has morphed into something unrecognizable. It's a murmuring throwback to former times, silky and strong at the same time and larded with mysterious jargon. Even girls from Kyoto are in the dark half the time, trying to guess what is under discussion as the geiko or maiko flit off in full regalia into the still-unknown world of the *ochaya* teahouses.

There is not a single chair or sofa around. She has to learn to sit on the tatami with her legs folded under her. This is called the *seiza* ("correct sitting") style. It is excruciating after the first twenty minutes, but unless she gets used to it, practicing tea ceremony is out of the question. She will have to sit this way at geisha parties in the future, too.

Her last duty of the day is to sit waiting in the entrance vestibule of the *okiya* for the geiko

Above: A geisha prepares for a performance. East Asian performers in many disciplines are expected to apply their own makeup. The act of doing so prepares one mentally to take on the role.

Right: A maiko preparing a traditional meal. Meals are not the focus of teahouse parties, but guests may order some exquisite morsels, which are delivered by *shidashi*, or outside caterers. The maiko is pouring sake from a *masu*, or square sake container.

and maiko to come back from the teahouses. This may be at one o'clock in the morning, or two, or later. Woe betide her if she isn't awake to greet her seniors properly. Then bath time. The Japanese bath is shaped like a deep cube, and filled to the brim with scalding hot water. You wash yourself outside it, on the guttered bathroom floor, then step in perfectly clean to soak in the water. Everyone uses the same water. So, everyone takes their bath in order of rank. The *shikomi* goes last, often as late as three o'clock in the morning. She will be up the next morning at six or seven. She may have to attend both the *kaburenjo* for practice in geisha arts and normal school. She gets two days off a month.

Backbreaking labor and sleep deprivation are part of every Japanese apprenticeship. In part, this is because the Ogasawara school of etiquette is of samurai origin. For all that Japan is proud of its uniquely pacifist constitution, which forbids the country to go to war, foreigners often remark on the militarist tone of life here. Uniforms abound; even kindergarten children line up in strict rows like soldiers on parade. The objective of *shikomi* training is the same as in military induction: to break and make a personality. This is why even today, the training is kept tough even though newcomers are such precious assets to the flower-and-willow world.

Eight months to a year of this is more than a lot of girls can stand. The rate of attrition is very high, and often goes over fifty percent. There are some lucky ones who don't have to pass through the *shikomi* stage at all. They may have been born into the house or come already trained in shamisen, dance, and comportment. But the majority of *okiya* have a *shikomi*, on her knees scrubbing, a domestic grub. Only the hope of turning into a butterfly keeps her going.

From *Minarai* to Maiko

The trainee typically finishes her *shikomi* period at about sixteen years of age. There is a formal, nerve-wracking test of her dancing ability at the *kaburenjo*, observed by an assortment of hanamachi grandees. Assuming she passes, she is now ready to become a fledgling maiko—a *minarai*. In line with the Japanese ideal of apprenticeship, the word literally means "looking and learning." This is a much shorter period in the training process, lasting only about a month or slightly longer, after which she will formally debut as an officially recognized maiko. She now adopts the appearance of one. Though we discuss geisha costume in detail in Chapter Five, we will take a quick look here at what this dramatic transformation entails.

Every aspect of the *minarai*'s and maiko's appearance is calculated to emphasize her beauty and seductiveness. Her hair is swept up in the dramatic *wareshinobu* style, wrapped around a red silk ribbon. Some maiko watchers (the *taikomochi* especially) go to great lengths to invest every aspect of the look with an erotic significance. The *wareshinobu*, with its central swathe of crimson surrounded by jet-black tresses, does not escape comment.

Every aspect of the maiko's appearance is calculated to emphasize her beauty and seductiveness.

Right: A geiko adjusting her wig.
Maiko never wear wigs, and geiko
only do so until they are about
thirty years old. Nor are wigs worn
to every performance or party.
Their use is restricted to more
formal occasions.

But the first thing that strikes the casual viewer is the forest of combs, flutters, hairpins, and silk bands that bedeck the head. The *minarai* carries about a dozen objects on her head. Many of them are related to the months and seasons. The *minarai* does not yet need a full set, because her term lasts only a month. What she does need to do, and quickly, is keep her head balanced. The whole ensemble may weigh three kilograms or more.

The face is a white mask of paint called *shironuri*. The effect of the facial makeup is electrifying. It immediately makes the wearer a uniquely powerful symbol of her art. Noh drama has its masks, which are actually more expressive; they are crafted with extreme subtlety to delineate a vast range of emotions when

skillfully tilted by the actors who wear them. The maiko's *shironuri* is a barrier marking her off as belonging to the flower-and-willow world, and it is a provocative contrast to the sensuous appeal of the rest of her costume. There is something here of the power of the *shirabyoshi*, a medieval dancer-shaman and a remote ancestor of the geisha. The effect is softened, but not overcome, by faint hints of blusher on her cheeks and around her eyes. Like a noh mask, the maiko's white face paint proclaims its artifice; a fraction is of the forehead and temples are left unpainted near the hairline, setting off the face even more as a work of art.

The facial features are marked out in vivid contrast. The eyes are rimmed with purple eyeliner, smudged out slightly at the corners to emphasize their perfect almond shape. The eyebrows are shaved and penciled in a similar shade. *Ryubi* is the Japanese word for the ideal shape—"willow brows." The mouth is a vivid leaf of crimson lipstick. At this early stage of her career, lipstick is applied only to the lower lip. The upper lip is painted white like the rest of the face, and is effectively invisible. It doesn't seem at all disconcerting to the Japanese eye, trained as it is to admire the tiny rosebud mouth of *ukiyo-e* art. For Westerners, it does take a bit of getting used to.

Earrings are conspicuous by their absence. The very idea of a geisha wearing them would send the collective flower-and-willow world rolling off its cushions and onto the tatami in hysterical laughter. For most of its history, earrings were taboo in Japan, as was piercing any

part of the body. The roots of this attitude seem to lie in Confucianism, which holds that making it to one's deathbed with one's body intact is a primary duty of thanks to one's parents, the authors of that body. "Why (as one older lady asked this writer) would you *want* to open a hole in your body that wasn't there when you were born?" The younger generation has abandoned this attitude. But the flower-and-willow world is not young.

The *minarai*'s upper chest and most of her shoulders are also made up in white. The unpainted strip of flesh follows the hairline, angles up behind the ears, then swoops down to the shoulder blades. Two tines of white slash up the nape, leaving a sharp "w" of unpainted flesh arrowing down from the hairline. The contrast between the sheer white makeup and the bare skin is the most blatantly erotic

Left: Back view of a geisha at New Year celebrations. Every traditional Japanese world, whether it be geisha, kabuki, or sumo, delights in preparing and presenting elaborate knots on costumes, envelopes, and hairstyles.

element of the flower-and-willow world's visual repertoire. The *taikomochi* school of symbolism has much to say about the "w" on the nape, which is for the Japanese the sexiest of all parts of the decently clothed body.

The maiko's kimono, called a *hikizuri*, is a quite different garment from the standard article. Fabrics are extremely costly; the line at the back of the neck hangs down outrageously low, all the better to reveal the nape. Here we find another potent symbol of the maiko—the *eri*, usually translated as "collar." It is a detachable bend of scarlet fabric sewn inside the inner top of the kimono neck. There it rests, plainly visible, the scarlet contrasting with the white-painted skin above. The kimono is bound with the *obi*, wrapped tightly from the chest to the abdomen. The pressure of the *obi* constricts movement like an old-fashioned European corset. Along with the layers of garments underneath, the whole ensemble can easily weigh twenty kilos. Teetering along in *okobo*

Right: A geisha's hair stylist attaches an elaborate wig to her client. Specialist wigmakers are now thin on the ground, and the costs they charge are exorbitant. Maiko have an even harder time; on average, they get their hair washed and reset only once a week.

clogs, with the head weighted with kilos more of ornaments, calls for great physical stamina. The *minarai*'s kimono train and *obi* are somewhat shorter than a proper maiko's, though, and so slightly lighter and less cumbersome.

Thus attired, the *minarai* is ready for action. Her main job is attending geisha parties (*ozashiki*) in the evening. At this stage of her career, all she is required to do is "look and learn." Rather like an actor at full-dress rehearsal, she starts to absorb the feel of the stage. The tatami room itself is now a familiar environment to her and she has learned how to sit properly for long stretches at a time. It feels different under the heavy fabrics and jewelry, however, and the month or so of *minarai* apprenticeship is the time available to learn how to move gracefully in full regalia. She studies the interaction of the other geiko in the room, some of whom will perhaps flit in and out for only a few minutes, and most of whom will have come from other *okiya*. There are grizzled old-timers and fresh young maiko. Each of them has their own network within the hanamachi, which has its cliques like every village. Some of them she knows from classes at the *kaburenjo*, and some she doesn't. After the relatively confined *shikomi* period, her social world within the hanamachi is widening. She is starting to form a network of her own. It will have to include both other maiko and gaiko, and guests who will call her to parties in the future.

Above all, there is the flow of chat, dances, and party games with the guests to get used to. How does each group of guests differ from the others? How do the geiko take care of

entertaining guests who are boring, or don't know much about the flower-and-willow world —or, in comparison guests who are practically part of the furniture? What happens when the guest of honor is a foreign businessman or celebrity who does not understand the Japanese language?

Above: The maiko's *hikizuke* kimono is one of Japan's most elaborate and expensive garments in secular use.

Above: A maiko with a mentor, possibly the Mother of an *ochaya* she is attending. In the early stages of their careers, maiko need a lot of advice and support.

Far right: A maiko in full regalia. Her hair is set in the *wareshinobu* style, and adorned with the November maple hairpin.

The *minarai* period is also when the apprentice gets her first look at how an *ochaya* works. Unlike other maiko and geiko, she does not attend parties at a lot of different establishments. Rather, she spends most of her working time at a single, set *ochaya*, called a *minarai-jaya* (the "o" in *ochaya* is an honorific; "jaya" is an aspirated form of "chaya.") Each geisha house, or *okiya*, tends to send their *minarai* to the same *ochaya* for initial training. The Mothers of each

establishment are close, and the *minarai-jaya* Mother keeps a close eye on the fledgling maiko. The girls can be very nervous at this early stage, and so they appreciate being watched out for and advised.

The *minarai* also gets to know the staff, especially the *nakai*, the servers of food and drinks. These are often older women, with long experience of hanamachi life. They are specialized professionals in themselves, kimono-clad and with their own style. The Kyoto *ochaya* pride themselves in offering the very best that Japanese entertaining can give. Nothing in the mix is allowed to deviate from the highest standards, the serving staff included. An uncompromising commitment to perfectionism is a feature of Japan in many walks of life; here, the *minarai* know that they are embarking on life at the very top level of their craft. No wonder they can feel nervous in this arena.

Maiko

The period of *minarai* training ends with a ceremony called *san-san-kudo*. It means "three-three-nine" and it constitutes a kind of wedding ceremony. As mentioned before, the idea of junior and senior plays a huge role the lives of people in Japan, and indeed all East Asia. The *san-san-kudo* ceremony turns the *minarai* into a maiko, and at the same time it formally binds her to an Older Sister. The Older Sister is a geiko, a fully qualified Kyoto geisha, and she normally comes from the same *okiya*. Their relationship in a sense is not new; they will have lived under the same roof for at least the best part of a year. During this time, the younger partner will have learned a lot from the older and will have depended on her for advice. But now she is being formally, publicly recognized as a partner in the same enterprise.

The ceremony is held on a lucky day (the hanamachi are very superstitious) either at the *minarai-jaya* or the *kemban*, depending on the district. The hanging scroll used in Ponto-cho depicts the Sun Goddess Amaterasu-o-mikami,

Right: Traditional Japanese footwear comes in a vast range of varieties, as the ultra-high clogs in the foreground attest. These performers were photographed during the 1950s.

as a reminder of the primal origins of dance in Japan. The ceremony is attended by the new maiko, her Older Sister, and geisha house Mother. In the places of honor sit the *minarai-jaya* Mother and the Older Sister's Older Sister —the new maiko's Great Older Sister. The president of the local Association of Teahouse Owners formally recognizes the bond, as does the president of the *kemban*.

The proceedings come to a climax with the ritual "three times three" exchange of thimble-sized cups of sake between the maiko and her Older Sister. Three cups are passed and each sipped three times. It is this action which bonds them. Sake is a sacred as well as a profane drink, and it plays a part in Shinto ritual rather like wine in Christianity. Shinto marriages are enacted with just the same three times three exchange. The sense of vocation is very pronounced in Japanese culture, and many people consider it an ideal to be literally married to the job. All kinds of professions have some kind of ceremonial for new entrants. Newly qualified nurses, for example, walk between two ranks of their comrades, who hold lighted candles—another clear allusion to the wedding ceremony as it is practiced in Japan. The new maiko's *san-san-kudo*, then, is far from being just a registration procedure. It's a very moving event, and it is not at all rare for tears to be shed. The maiko takes on a new name at this point, half of it adopted from her Older Sister's name. She is becoming, in a real sense, part of the family.

Being part of the family means that any problems caused by the maiko—absences from classes or rehearsals, failure to observe ritualized greetings—are the concern of her *okiya* and a question of her *okiya*'s standing. Part of an Older Sister's job is to take the heat. In Japanese senior-junior relationships, the junior's conduct

is the senior's responsibility. This is not as pressing as it may sound; you aren't held responsible if a kindergarten junior robs a bank in later life. It does hold true in closed hierarchies like companies, though, and a geisha district is a dense network of closed hierarchies, all rubbing together. The Older Sister will smooth things over if, for example, a maiko neglects to pay a thank-you call to the Mother of an *ochaya* she had called to for a party. For the maiko, the Older Sister is like a coach in the applied etiquette of hanamachi life.

Though the geisha district are thinning out and becoming less intense, the Older Sister figure is still a key builder of political networks. Most geiko collect as many Younger Sisters as they can throughout their careers. Those Younger Sisters in turn acquire Younger Sisters,

Left: A group of geisha being instructed by their tea ceremony teacher, 1955. The woman second from right may be smiling out of amusement, or out of embarrassment at some minor lapse of decorum.

Right: Older and younger rely on each other, building up a supportive network in the hanamachi.

building up a pyramid of support and protection and a wedge of power in the hanamachi. Many vital decisions are out of the hands of the geiko themselves—who takes lead roles in the annual Cherry Dances, for example, or which young maiko should appear on this season's promotional poster. The *kemban*, the Teahouse Owner's Association, and the more influential of the *ochaya* and *okiya* Mothers all have a say in these matters. But a powerful support network of Older Sisters and Great Older Sisters will give a newly qualified maiko more leverage as she starts out.

The junior-senior relationship cuts both ways, however, and the attentions of an Older Sister and the others can be oppressive as well as supportive; the Older Sister will expect to have a say in every aspect of a maiko's life, however personal. These days, some maiko try

to make do without one. What they gain in independence, however, they can easily lose to hostile criticism. The hanamachi is a tightly knit village indeed.[35]

The day after the *san-san-kudo* ceremony is another formative event—the maiko's formal debut, or *misedashi* ("Opening for Business.") This is as public as the *san-san-kudo* is private. Envelopes advertising the upcoming debut are put up throughout the hanamachi; they are returned with lavish tips. Even the general public are in on it. On the morning of her debut, the street outside her *minarai-jaya* is thronged with the amateur photographers who attend in their droves every event, every festival, every happening however remarkable or mundane in the country. The *Kyoto Shimbun* newspaper will be there. If a maiko is known to be exceptionally beautiful, talented, or well-connected, the TV stations may even make an appearance. There may be stars of the kabuki stage, and other dignitaries connected with the flower-and-willow world. There will be family, too, from the maiko's birth family, both proud and a bit alarmed at the transformation in their daughter.

The moment arrives; the door of the teahouse opens. With pride in her achievement butterflies in her stomach, the new maiko steps out to the clatter of camera shutters. She is accompanied by her Older Sister or perhaps by an *otokosu*, a male dresser. The entrance is decorated with *mokuroku*, celebratory hand-painted posters. She then makes a grand tour of the hanamachi, stopping off at the various *ochaya* and restaurants, offering ceremonial greetings and receiving ceremonial and usually heartfelt congratulations. The advent of a new maiko is an occasion of joy for the whole geisha district. It is proof that, whatever the difficulties of keeping the operation going, life does go on. The new maiko will contribute to the tone of the geisha district as a whole, and if she becomes a star, she will contribute to its finances as a whole. While there may be fierce competition among individual maiko and geiko, the hanamachi itself is tightly interwoven. It survives—and has survived hard times in the past—only through this spirit of mutual aid and interdependence.

The three days of the debut are a blur of greetings, visits, and parties in the evening. Wearing a formal, black-crested kimono, she performs in the *ochaya* for the first time. In keeping with the *iki* approach to money and its use, the maiko gathers a fortune in celebratory

tips. It is so exhausting that many maiko apparently retain only very vague memories of their *misedashi* and the days following. She certainly needs a break at this point, but may be lucky to get it. She is now a "dance-child" (*mai-ko*), a fully functioning member of the flower-and-willow world.

Although the maiko has gone up a decisive rung in the hierarchy of the hanamachi, her days are scarcely less busy then the lowly *shikomi* apprentice. Her mornings are still taken up with dance and music classes at the *kaburenjo*. She is also expected to practice tea ceremony. *Ozashiki* start around six o'clock, and keep her occupied until the small hours. Her

Above: Is she making the Western gesture for "perfect" or the Japanese gesture for "money?" In either case, her elders seem quite amused.

performance style will be starting to mature, but no one expects her to have mastered the fine art of trivial conversation yet. In fact, in days gone by, most *ochaya* regulars rather preferred maiko to be wallflowers. Shy, mumbled replies interspersed with self-conscious giggles are a major weapon in the armory of *kawaii*, the aesthetic of cute naiveté that has gone on to conquer modern Japan. These days, however, maiko are becoming much more self-confident and assertive at *ozashiki* parties, and much quicker to emulate the wit and repartee of the geiko. They are very much the stars of the hanamachi, and being constantly feted soon builds up their sense of confidence and self-mastery.

While certain standards are still fairly relaxed for maiko, they are fully responsible for their faces and hair. They have to make up their own faces, and they put a lot of effort into getting it correct and consistent from day to day. Retouching the makeup is almost impossible, and besides, they don't have the time to redo it over and over. Their hairstyles are another trial, and even more troublesome. Because they are so elaborate and expensive to create, they can't be rearranged every day. The norm is a visit to the hairdressers just once a week. As a result,

Right: Higher artistic standards are expected each step of the way through apprenticeship. Trainees receive a lesson in the proper way to handle a fan from an older geisha.

they have to sleep on high wooden pillows, which are very uncomfortable. These are softened by a small cushion attached to the top, but it is very easy for the maiko's head to slip off the pillow in her sleep, in which case the hairstyle is ruined. One is a maiko twenty-four hours a day.

There is another major call on a maiko's time. From the moment she debuts, she is propelled into the great annual round of public performances, festivals, and events that so distinguish the city of Kyoto. Rehearsals for the Cherry Dances, for example, may last six very busy weeks. Trying to combine all that with the daily routine is very wearing. However, this is what maiko have signed up for, and the vast majority of them naturally revel in the glamour.

This round of events steeps the new maiko in an awareness of the seasons—even more so than the typical Japanese person, which is saying a lot. The national and local event calendar is only one of the many things that does so. Wisteria in May, hydrangea in June, morning glory in August—from the hairpins she wears to the kimonos and other accessories, her outfit follows the seasons. It is almost impossible to over-emphasize the impact of the seasonal cycle on the life of the maiko and geiko. The foods the guests eat at parties, the flower arrangements and hanging scrolls add to that awareness. If she practices haiku, she chooses seasonal keywords with care.

Sadly, it is often the case that the more the new maiko is a professional success, the harder her personal life becomes. If a newcomer on the scene earns too much, gets too many plum roles

Above: A geisha's hair stylist combs a wig for her client.

at performances, or too high a profile in tourism advertising spreads, she had better watch out. There can be a lot of resentment and back-stabbing in this pressure-cooker environment. Iwasaki Mineko's rise in 1960s Gion Kobu was meteoric. She paid a high price:

> The hostility took many forms; some were crueler than others. For example, my props and accessories (fans, parasols, tea whisks, etc.) were constantly disappearing. Other geiko were rude or ignored me at banquets. People called the *okiya* and left messages purposely misdirecting me to appointments.

Right: Iwasaki Mineko at the height of her career. Her memoirs detail years of harassment and ostracism at the hands of her fellow maiko and geiko. The problem was especially severe in Iwasaki's case because her Older Sister (who was also her biological sister) hated her intensely. Iwasaki was thus deprived of the protective web of personal connections needed to protect hanamachi insiders from resentment and rivalry.

The hem of a maiko's kimono is padded with batting to give the train its proper heft and shape. One night someone stuck needles into the padding. After being pricked innumerable times, I went home and sadly pulled twenty-two needles out of the hem of my beautiful kimono. [36]

Of course, maiko and geiko make lifelong friendships in the hanamachi also. Iwasaki's treatment was especially severe because she lacked a political support network. Her Older Sister, who was in fact her biological sister, hated her intensely. The hatred was mutual. The ostracism and harassment lasted for years. Iwasaki eventually struck back with a rumor, hinting here and there that her sister was undergoing psychiatric care. 1960s Japan still had a strong stigma attached to mental illness, so this was a devastating tactic. Like all rumors, it swept the hanamachi like wildfire.

Up to the 1940s and 1950s, the next step in most maiko's careers was *mizuage*, or losing her virginity. As already discussed, the sexual partner might be a *mizuage danna* who she had never met before and might never meet again,

Left: A maiko en route to a party to entertain guests with singing and dancing. Much of the Kyoto streetscape used to consist of elegant, dignified townhouses such as these. A few pockets remain, drowned in mediocre modern architecture.

Above: For all the tensions and rivalries, lifelong friendships are formed in the hanamachi.

and the event was a commercial transaction. In other cases, if a regular *danna* patron had already been arranged, she slept with him. There was no concealing the event. In fact, to the great embarrassment of most maiko, it was proclaimed to all and sundry by a change in her hairstyle. The *wareshinobu* style was replaced by the *ofuku,* a slightly less elaborate style with less ornamentation. The appearance of the *ofuku* hairdo was the occasion for congratulations on the street. The maiko was now a woman.

Now that *mizuage* is a thing of the past, the switchover to the *ofuku* style simply proclaims that one has become a senior maiko. It is usually adopted around the age of eighteen. *Okobo*

straps change color from red to pink, and later to purple. She now wears the *katsuyama* hairstyle during the Gion Festival in July. This is a name which reaches right back into the past, as it is named for the legendary eighteenth century *tayu* courtesan from the Yoshiwara pleasure district. For the last month of her life as a maiko, she adopts the *sakko* hairstyle, which is a very elaborate bouffant. Some maiko now revert to the past in a way which is utterly unique in modern Japan: they have their teeth blackened. Long banned from the imperial court, the only other people who uphold this practice are the actor-courtesans of the Shimabara district. The teeth remain blackened until the maiko changes her status and becomes a geiko.

If she so chooses, the senior maiko is now ready to become a fully-fledged Kyoto geiko. Her skills have been arduously built up along with her network of contacts and clients. She is about twenty years old, and has been living and training in the flower-and-willow world for five years or longer.

As of the early 2000s, there are between fifty and sixty maiko in all of Kyoto.

Geiko

Many entrants to the Kyoto hanamachi decide to call it a day at this point. They have absorbed enough of the unique spririt of the Kyoto flower-and-willow world to make more than an adequate living in the world of refined *asobi* anywhere in Japan. The classiest bars of the Ginza are waiting with widespread arms. A few of the girls have already decided to marry and settle down, often with partners from the elite of the sports or political worlds. The latter in particular will be grateful for the wealth of contacts which their ex-maiko spouses can provide.

For those who have decided to go on, the hanamachi awaits in all its claustrophobic glory. The ceremony which makes an adult geiko of the maiko is called *erikae:* the changing of the collar. The scarlet maiko collar is one of the treasured symbols of the younger apprentice geiko; as time passes, it is appliqued in silver thread. By the time the moment comes for the maiko to become a geiko, the scarlet has been almost buried under the silver. It is time for the transition from trainee to master.

The *erikae* ceremony involves the same round of formal calls round the district's *ochaya*, *okiya,* and *ryotei* as the *misedashi.* The scarlet collar, so long a symbol of the sheer eroticism of the maiko, is unstitched and replaced with a white one. The one-time raw recruit is no longer a girl, and no longer expected to make it on looks alone. From now on, her power of personality and performance skills will earn her living. This is provided she has built up the correct customer base and an adequate support network.

Geiko dress is much more conservative than the sumptuous maiko look. The kimono neckline no longer hangs down quite so provocatively to the shoulder blades. Younger geiko wear wigs; while decorated with hairpins made of jade or coral, their coiffure is not the fantastic confection gracing the heads of the maiko. The platform *okobo* clogs give way to

Left: The nape is a highly erogenous zone in Japanese sexuality. The white makeup serves to conceal, reveal, and tantalize.

less flamboyant *zori* sandals and *geta* clogs. This does not mean that geisha are dowdy—not in the slightest. Their style, deportment, and sophistication are a world apart from the norm, and instantly recognizable. Exceptional standards of artistry, etiquette, and poise are demanded of the geiko. They are no longer maiko, and allowances are no longer made for slight lapses of concentration or gaps in knowledge of the repertoire.

With the exception of Miyagawa-cho, geiko are now firmly established in specialized roles as *tachikata* (dancers) and *jikata* (musicians). *Tachikata* tend to be more beautiful, and the stars among them are in constant demand. Their schedules may be booked up many months in advance, and they may spend only short periods of time at each party. Flitting through the evening from one *ochaya* to the next, they build up very substantial earnings and tips. A geisha's time is charged in units, from five to thirty minutes depending on the hanamachi. But guests are expected to pay a full fee for a geiko who spends any time at all

Right: Maiko become increasingly confident in their artistic and social prowess as their training develops. This photograph was taken in 1965.

The main kimono is patterned
according to the season; the less
decoration, the more senior the
geisha. All Kyoto geisha wear black
crested kimonos to very formal
events. The *obi* (sash) is worn over
the *obi-age*, which helps keep it in
position. The narrow braid worn
over the *obi* is called the *obi-jime*.
The normal footwear is *zori* sandals.

The main undergarment is the *nagajuban*, a full-length under-kimono that follows the same line as the garment over it. A collar or *eri* is stitched on. Geiko (fully-qualified Kyoto geisha) *nagajuban* are pink or other light, pastel colors.

The main undergarment is the nagajuban, a full-length under-kimono that follows the same line as the garment over it. A collar or eri is stitched on. Geiko (fully-qualified Kyoto geisha) nagajuban are pink or other light, pastel colors.

The *hadajuban* resembles a buttonless blouse. It is worn right side folded over left, as with all traditional Japanese clothes. The slip covering the legs is popularly known as a *susoyoke*.

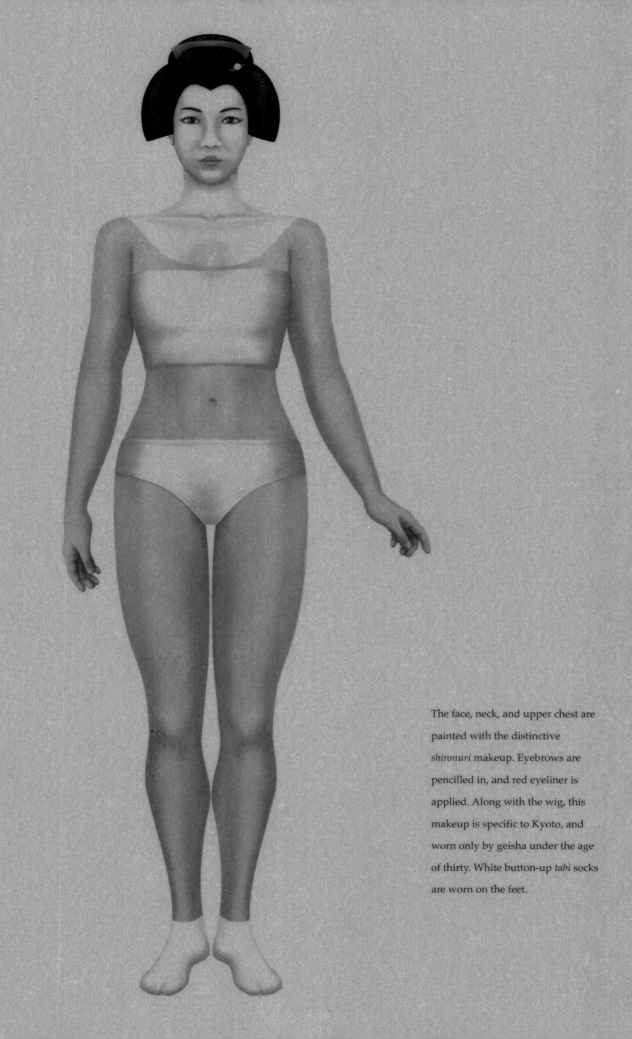

The face, neck, and upper chest are painted with the distinctive *shironuri* makeup. Eyebrows are pencilled in, and red eyeliner is applied. Along with the wig, this makeup is specific to Kyoto, and worn only by geisha under the age of thirty. White button-up *tabi* socks are worn on the feet.

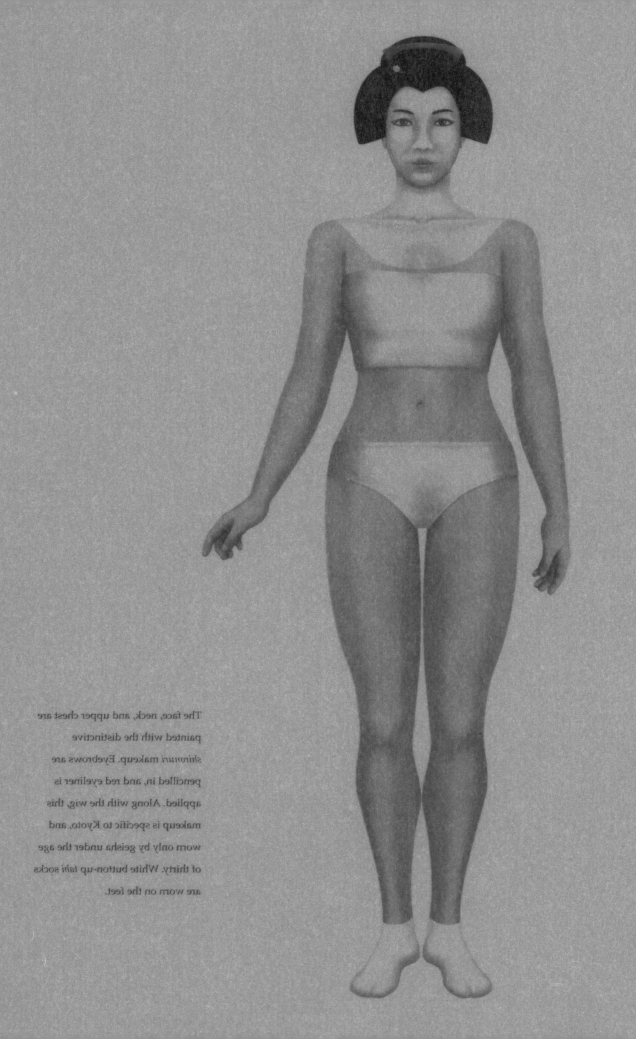

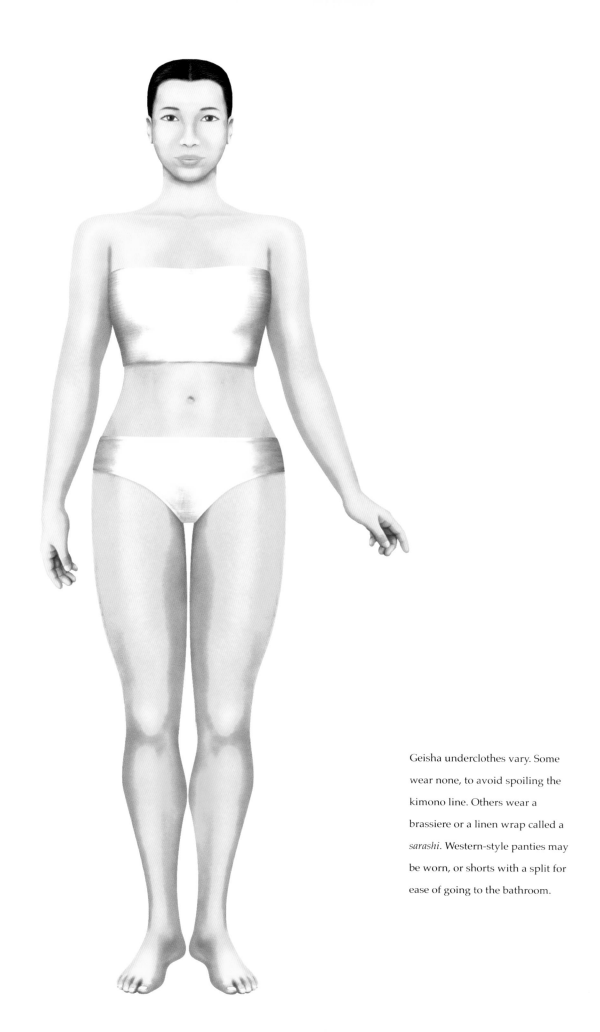

Geisha underclothes vary. Some wear none, to avoid spoiling the kimono line. Others wear a brassiere or a linen wrap called a *sarashi*. Western-style panties may be worn, or shorts with a split for ease of going to the bathroom.

Right: This photograph was taken during a cherry blossom festival at the Brooklyn Botanic Gardens in New York.

Far right: A professional playing Japan's most esoteric role for women. Her hair is decorated with the August hairpin, depicting *eulalia* (Japanese pampas grass).

at a party. So, the more parties attended, the higher the earnings.

Jikata tend to earn somewhat less, but theirs is a steady profession. The set-up of an *ozashiki* party requires both dancers and musicians. Elderly *jikata*, being really expert players of the shamisen, are in strong demand. The fate everyone wants to avoid is to be left for the evening, sitting in "grinding tealeaves into powder" (*ocha-ohiku*). This undignified state involves being all dressed up but having no invitations to any of the *ochaya*.

The geiko is by now an expert reader of the hanamachi scene. The *ochaya* in particular is a highly legible environment for her, and she begins to decode it the moment she arrives for an engagement. A glance at the racks of shoes at the entrance will tell her how many guests

are around, how many of them are men or women, and how stylish they are. She will probably recognize some regular customers' shoes. The tatami room where the party is being held will be a mine of information from the millisecond she enters it, sliding the paper door open in impeccable Ogasawara fashion. What hanging scroll is on display? What kind of incense is being used? Has the teahouse seen fit to put out its very best tableware, or are the guests not quite so important in the scheme of things? There may already be other geiko or maiko sitting in the room. One of them may be a new maiko who visited her *okiya* during her debut. A glance is enough to establish how she is bearing up in her new status. One of them is wearing a kimono which was obviously a gift from so-and-so. What does this say about her relationship with the donor, and by implication her network of Older Sisters and Great Older Sisters? All of these considerations, among others, may be in play as the geiko approaches the guest of honor and trills how simply delighted she is to meet him (or, less frequently, her.) By this stage of her career, the geiko is saturated in the life and lore of the hanamachi. She is cheerful and confident as the shamisen strikes up, a professional playing Japan's most esoteric role for women.

The *Taikomochi* Tradition

The male geisha tradition is on the verge of extinction. There are no specialized schools for the profession, and never have been. Maiko go into mountains of debt to become geiko. Traditionally, *taikomochi* did also—by bankrupting themselves on carousing in the hanamachi until there was nothing for it but to turn professional. Most come into the hanamachi with a deep knowledge of traditional music and dance, and strong connections with the world of *rakugo* storytelling. Yugentei Tamasuke was a good example. His father, a sake salesman, used to sneak off to afternoon kabuki shows under the pretext of making deliveries, and he would take the young Tamasuke with him. Yugentei eventually apprenticed with a *rakugo* artist, living under the same roof, before eventually becoming a licensed *taikomochi*. The training was essentially on the job; his background was such that no formal course was necessary.

CHAPTER 4

the day of a geisha

The hanamachi streets are relatively quiet until after four o'clock, when preparations for the evening's parties begin.

Right: A geisha looking out of a window of a teahouse.

Far right: These geisha, photographed in 1965, are intently practising *taiko* drumming.

Geisha are we, bidden to be
Present today at the ceremonee

Hall and Greenback, *The Geisha, a story of a teahouse*, 1896

The Learning Curve: Morning

Japan is a nation of early risers. Children assemble in parks during their summer holidays to do group calisthenics, starting at six in the morning. Nothing could be further from the spirit of the flower-and-willow world. But even though they work late into the night, the maiko and geiko of Kyoto are up in reasonable time. The maiko in particular get to classes as early as possible. The best teachers will be available for the first comers. For older geiko, nine o'clock is commendable and ten o'clock reasonable. While they don't eat at the evening *ozashiki* parties, geisha are allowed to drink and some of them may be slightly groggy, or worse. The *shikomi* apprentices at the bottom of the pecking order will have been up for hours, have finished their morning chores, and perhaps headed off to class at regular junior high school. In Kyoto, geiko who live in *okiya* do not touch housework and are not expected to. Their income keeps the whole ship afloat.

Even in Kyoto, however, many geisha do not wake up in an *okiya*, but in their own apartments. Kyoto geisha are typically contracted to the *okiya* which trained them for between five and seven years. During this period, they gradually pay back the money that has been invested in their training and costumes. They are then free to become *jimae geiko*—independent artists, living on their own. They still retain very close links with their original *okiya*, however. All invitations to *ozashiki* are routed through the *okiya*, so they still have to call in every working day to confirm their appointments and head out for the evening from there.

Right: An exterior shot of typical housing in Kyoto. The spire of a Buddhist pagoda peeps up among the TV aerials on the right.

The trade-off for *jimae geiko* is between freedom and security. They are now independent, but their *okiya* will no longer cover the exorbitant costs of staying in business. A basic set of costumes with accessories will cost at the very least five million yen—over a year's salary for an ordinary Joe. This is just the beginning. Her stock of kimonos and *obi* will have to be constantly expanded to maintain the required image. She can't afford to live cheaply. The restaurants she goes to must be among the best in town; whenever she travels, it has to be first class. Ideally, somebody else will be paying, but even if it's out of her own purse, standards must be maintained. Anything else would be simply not *iki*.

Geisha have to be careful and lucky, therefore, not to wake up to a massive financial headache. In the old days, a *danna* took care of all the expenses. This is rather rare these days. Instead, popular geiko tend to be supported by groups of clients who act like fan clubs. There may be an *obi danna*, who will pay for sashes, and so on. Many women have comfortable lives, while some struggle from season to season. There is a strong sense of vocation among geiko; they have to be really committed to the profession and the life. The excitement and beauty of hanamachi life is unparalleled, but there is little security in the flower-and-willow world. A geiko has to continually hone her skills.

Classes take place in large tatami rooms. On arrival, maiko and geiko first make the rounds to formally greet their seniors. *Jikata* concentrate on the shamisen, flute, and percussion instru-

ments: *taiko* (a large drum plated with drumsticks); *kotsuzumi* (a smaller drum held up on the right shoulder and struck with the hand); and the *ohkawa* (a slightly larger drum, held on the lap). The range of instruments is the same as in noh drama.

The artistic symbol of geisha craft is the shamisen. It is popular outside the hanamachi too, but a geisha party would be simply

Above: A geisha playing the *fue* (flute).

unimaginable without it. Geisha are even nick-named "cats" not because of their independence and mystery, but because cat skin is used to cover the front of the instrument. The shamisen is older than the flower-and-willow world, and it evokes an older aesthetic known as *shibui*—spare, astringent, and closer to *wabi* (the tea ceremony aesthetic) than *iki* (the hana-machi aesthetic). Yet it serves its turn as a raiser of spirits also. "Throaty" is perhaps the best word to describe the twang of a shamisen string. It has its peculiar flavor—indeed, the word *shibui* covers sensations like biting into an unripe fruit like persimmon. It is an acquired but permanent taste for the instrument's many fans and players.

There are many styles of shamisen music, accompanied by singing or recitation. The best known is the *kouta* ("small song"). It fits in well with the flower-and-willow world because it is comparatively short, upbeat, and amusing—ideal for evening parties. *Nagauta* ("long song") is a more traditional ballad style dating back to the days of the shogunate, and connected to the kabuki style of theater. One of the most interesting styles is *gidayu*, which comes from *bunraku*, the Japanese puppet theater. In marked contrast to the West, puppetry has always been accepted as one of the major art forms, and has left a major mark on traditional music and on kabuki, which adapted many of its plots for the human stage. Its influence on the flower-and-willow world was thus double, directly through shamisen playing (especially in the *gidayu* style) and indirectly through kabuki, which impacted on dance styles.

Left: Geisha playing *otsuzumi* (first and second from left) and *kotsuzumi*, under the watchful eye of an instructor, visible on the far right.

Nihon buyo is a stately, graceful dance form in which even an elderly expert practitioner can appear as ravishingly beautiful as the freshest young maiko. The same transformation is at work on the kabuki stage, where men who could easily pass for corporate middle managers tread the boards as heartrendingly exquisite tragic heroines—and very convincingly, too, for any viewer trained in the conventions of the form. Like kabuki, *Nihon buyo* is a classical art form, in the sense that mere self-expression is not the aim. The emphasis is on the perfect execution of set forms (*kata*). Like classical pianists, however, the more one matures in the art, the more powerful the performance becomes. This is one reason why *tachikata* geisha do not need to retire young, and why the image of the geisha as simply a "Japanese dancing girl" is so inadequate.

In addition to music and dance, tea ceremony, calligraphy, flower arranging, and haiku and *waka* poetry are also on the hanamachi curriculum. Special rehearsal periods for annual dance events are common. Discipline is not so strict as in the old days, but both maiko and geiko are expected to be committed professionals in maintaining and developing their skills. In fact, they take great pride in being taught by some of the best teachers in the country. The equivalent of Master status in Japanese dance is called *natori* ("taking a name"). Like all traditional arts, mastery requires long periods of practice. Even *natori* are not permitted to become professional teachers, however; they are streamed through different courses from the beginning of their careers.

Right: Geisha are experts in performance and feel very at home in the theater.

In Gion Kobu, the *tachikata* (dance) maiko and geiko study a form of unmasked noh dance called *shimai*. There are other factors to the Inoue style, though. There are historical influences reaching all the way back to the *shirabyoshi* dancers. It is notable that the second head of the school, Inoue Aya, studied and absorbed *bunraku* as well as noh during the early nineteenth century.[37] The other Kyoto hanamachi have their dominant styles, with more influences from kabuki: Fujima in Gion Higashi, Onoue in Ponto-cho, Wakayagi in Miyagawa-cho, and Hanayagi in Kamishichiken. *Nihon buyo* has a nationwide following, and is not confined only to the flower-and-willow and kabuki worlds.

The Learning Curve, Continued: Afternoon

With classes over, the afternoon begins. This is a quiet time in the hanamachi, with most of the activity taking place in the *okiya*. Lunch is usually the main meal of the day for geisha, because they cannot eat at the *ozashiki* parties, and prefer a light meal just before them, especially if they are *tachikata*.

Afternoon is a time when many geisha catch up on current affairs. Many Japanese people pay little attention to the news, national or international. Higher standards are expected of the geisha in the classiest hanamachi, because they entertain the movers and shakers of Japanese politics and industry. There may also be foreign guests, though few geisha speak anything but hanamachi dialect Japanese.

Geisha also read up on specific people—the guests who have booked parties in advance. These are the ones who select geisha to attend. They are often people in the news, so geisha go through back issues of newspapers and magazines. They may even drop in to a public library. Any scrap of information can be turned to account, to liven up a conversation or steer away from topics that might be embarrassing. If a guest is boring or taciturn, background research can be a lifesaver. Also, though the geisha know in advance who is booking the party, they do not know the guest of honor or other participants. Research helps the geisha to understand the people they are entertaining.

Afternoon visits to *ochaya* Mothers and other members of the hanamachi take up time,

Left: Maiko participate in a tea ceremony at Kitano Shrine in the Kami Shichiken district.

and there is other work for everyone depending on their position in the geisha world. The *shikomi*, having finished their morning chores, at last have time to attend their dance lessons. The trainee maiko are also occupied with visits and practice. They are also traditionally expected to tidy up their seniors' dressing tables. Some of the veteran geisha, trusted by everyone in the hanamachi, are on the local board of the Geisha Association. They may use what spare time they have in the afternoon to attend meetings, liase with the Association of Teahouse Owners and other authorities, and consult with other geisha about any difficulties they may be having.

Even so, the hanamachi streets are relatively quiet until after four o'clock, when preparations

for the evening's parties begin. Things now start to liven up considerably. The *okiya* turn into hives of activity. Newly qualified maiko struggle with their makeup, trying to apply the thick white face paint in just the same way as they did the day before. Their napes are made up using stencils to get the distinctive bare "w" just right. Geiko check their hairstyles, or may break out their wigs if the occasion is a particularly formal one. If they are still under thirty, they may also put on the white *shironuri* make-up. Everyone goes through the *okiya*'s stockpile of kimonos and other accessories, paying careful attention to the season, the occasion, and

how all the elements of the costume are going to match. In Gion Kobu, the last surviving *otokosu* (male dressers) are at the peak of their day, rushing from *okiya* to *okiya* to help the geisha put on the outer layers of their costumes, and tie the *obi*. It is backbreaking work. These days, dressers are more usually women. Given the lack of opportunities, men have voted with their feet and deserted the hanamachi. It is a bizarre mirror image of Japan's usual gender discrimination.

As the *okiya* performers prepare for launch, the independent *jimae geiko* trail in from their apartments, bearing their own equipment. The *okiya* becomes another mirror-image, this time of a center of military operations. Although the outline schedule for the evening has been set in advance, the details are still being firmed up.

Teams of geisha need to be formed—in Kyoto maiko, and geiko of both *jikata* and *tachikata* varieties. Which dancer would go best with which shamisen player for this party? Who is going to do most of the talking, and where can a maiko be found for this teahouse? The hanamachi goes into overdrive, with telephone calls bouncing from *okiya* to *okiya* to *ochaya* and back. Gion Kobu even installed its own private telephone system for the purpose, back in the 1960s. These days, every geisha's bag contains a mobile phone, so the evening's movements can be controlled with more finesse as the need arises. But, barring the unforeseen, the schedule for the operation has to be set before six, when the *ozashiki* parties start.

Left: Achieving a consistent face each day is a difficult task for younger maiko. This artist applies lipstick to her lower lip, signifying that she is more than a year into her apprenticeship. The artifice of the geisha look is emphasized by the unpainted strip along the hairline.

Opposite page, top: An exterior shot of a traditional window in the Gion quarter. The paper window-pane is tinted blue.

Opposite page, bottom: Maiko go through their tea ceremony paces before a group of hanamachi dignitaries. The servers in red are *nakai*, professional hanamachi insiders with their own exacting standards of conduct and deportment.

Right: In the Kami Shichiken district of Kyoto near Kitano, geiko Tamayuki and a friend welcome customers. She is gracefully performing a set movement or *kata*.

Ozashiki: The Evening

Ozashiki in standard Japanese simply means an area for entertaining guests which has a tatami matting floor and low tables. The flower-and-willow world uses it in this way too, but the word also covers the party itself. What the world at large sees are the spectacular dance performances laid on for the public, but the *ozashiki* is the private heart of the geisha world. The *ozashiki* party is precisely what the profession was born to do, and it is essentially unchanged since the mid-eighteenth century.

The quotation from the musical by Hall and Greenback at the start of the chapter is a very early use of the word "geisha" in English and it is quite exact: geisha are "bidden" to be present. [38] They are very aware that their world would evaporate without the guests. But neither trainees nor qualified geisha behave like underlings. They are playfully polite, but not fawning. They enter and greet the guests formally, and at first sit near the door, the lowest honorific position in the room. But very soon they start to move around, pouring flasks of sake, chatting with the guests, and accepting drinks themselves.

They speak in an intermediate level between the familiar and the extremely polite. Many of the guests are used to being addressed in the latter style all day by flunkies and dogsbodies at work. The flower-and-willow world is never so tame. Most male guests are addressed as *o-niisan* ("Big Brother")—a perfectly common form of casual address in Japanese. Failing that, they may be called *shassan*, which is something

along the lines of the British English "guv'nor." Older personages are commonly *otoh-san*, "Father." What guests are never called by is their real name, no matter how many times they have met the same geisha. Nicknames are used for regulars. By chance their names might

Above: The entrance curtain (*noren*) of a teahouse in Gion, carrying the logo of the establishment. The curtains at the entrance were firstly contrived as sunshades, but became signs for the wares within.

be overheard in the next room, and many guests don't want it to be known that they spend time in the hanamachi, or that they are there that particular evening.

There may be only one guest, or four or five. There will be at least two geisha, usually more. In Kyoto, maiko are in heavy demand, so they and the stars among the geiko may drop in for shorter periods. Proceedings begin with a formal toast and light conversation. The *tachikata* then dance to the music of the shamisen, accompanied by the maiko if they are present. The dances are brief and fairly simple, usually only two or three minutes long. The performers do requests when asked. For the very few guests who still have a deep understanding of the traditional culture, it is difficult to say which brings the more pleasure—enjoying the performers' sophistication and wit, or savoring their beauty and skill in music and dance. So much of what the Japanese themselves consider finest in their own culture is on display simultaneously. In the less elite hanamachi, the dances and costumes (indeed the

Right: Pouring sake is a social ritual in itself. No one pours for oneself in polite company. Geisha may not eat during parties, but they are permitted to drink.

The *obi* (sash) is tied in a distinctive
boxy knot, which differentiates
fully-qualified Kyoto geisha (geiko)
from trainees (maiko) at a glance.

The *obi* (sash) is tied in a distinctive
boxy knot, which differentiates
fully-qualified Kyoto geisha (geiko)
from trainees (maiko) at a glance.

The *nagajuban* is a full-length
undergarment with an attached
collar which is visible under the
kimono proper.

The nagajuban is a full-length
undergarment with an attached
collar which is visible under the
kimono proper.

The *hadajuban* blouse is worn over

the *susoyoke* slip.

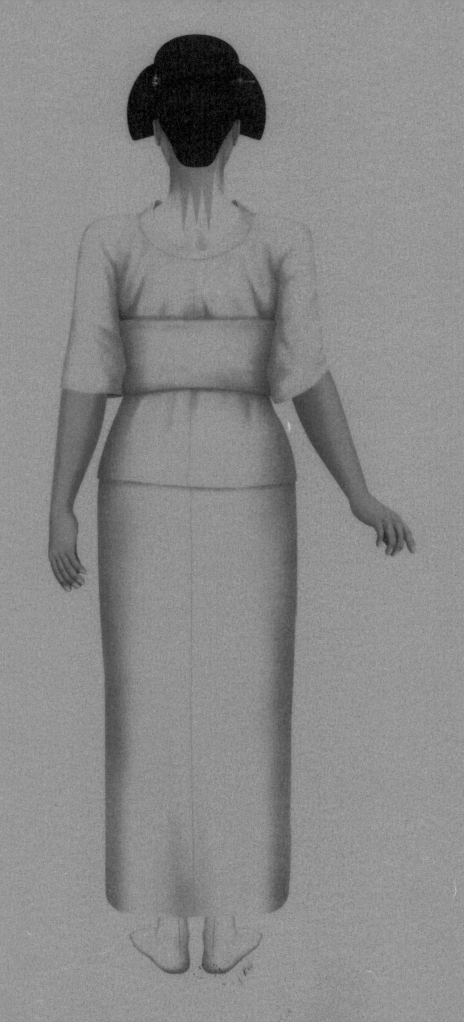

The hadajuban blouse is worn over the susoyoke slip.

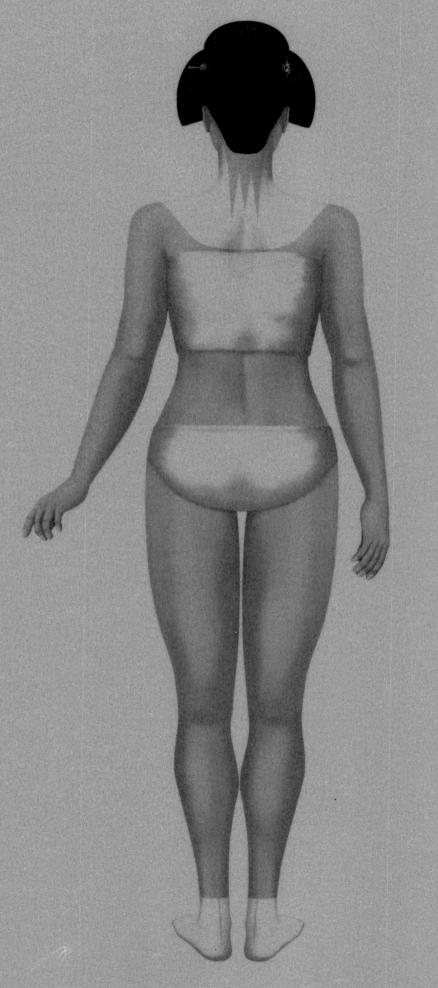

Two lines of skin are left unpainted
at the back of the neck, or three for
more formal occasions.

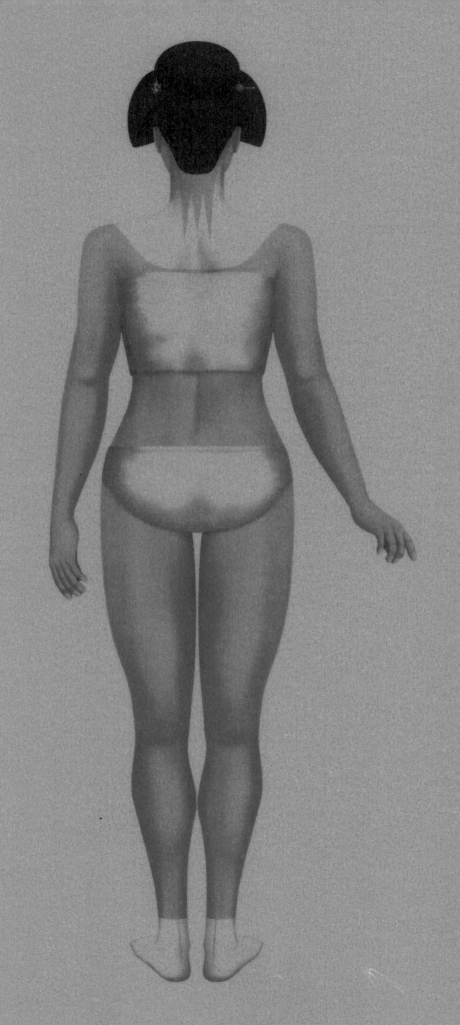

Two lines of skin are left unpainted
at the back of the neck, or three for
more formal occasions.

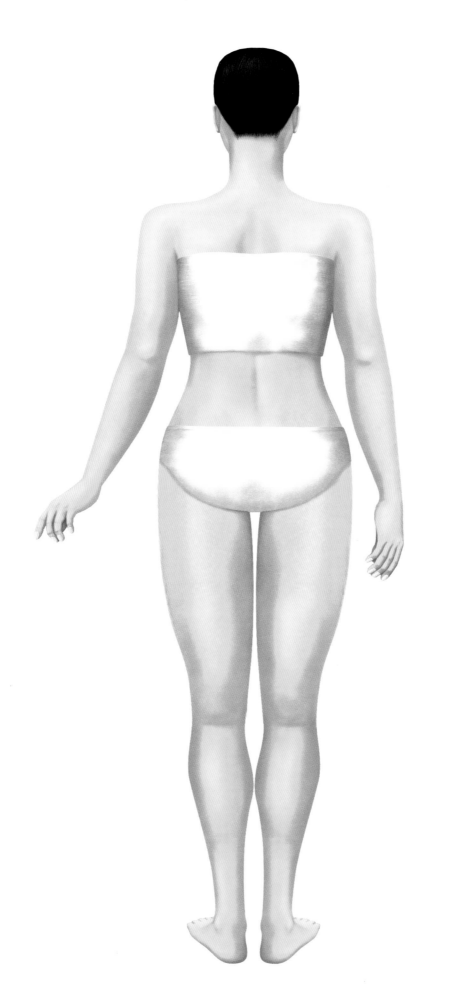

The chest is covered with a linen *sarashi* wrap, though brassieres may be worn, or nothing. Western-style panties or more traditional undergarments may be worn.

whole lifestyle) may be simpler, but here too the performers do their best to make the guests feel like princes (or occasionally princesses.)

Eating is not a major aspect of *ozashiki*, but the guests may order some exquisite and very expensive morsels, which are delivered to *ochaya* by *shidashi*, or caterers. As more sake, beer, or other alcohol is downed, the party may move on to drinking games. These are a part of many ordinary Japanese parties too, and the games at *ozashiki* are usually variants of familiar routines. But the *ozashiki* games have their own special flavor. Many of them are rooted in the past, and first-time guests may get an eerie sensation that they are stepping back in time. This is part of the effect the performers are aiming for. The following are some typical games:

Tora tora ("Tiger, tiger"): A geisha and guest are separated, kneeling on either side of a low screen. They adopt a pose indicating a tiger, a hunter, or a landowner. Each simultaneously leans forward and peers around at the other player. The hunter kills the tiger; the tiger eats the landowner; the landowner pockets the hunter's money. This is a variation of the scissors-paper-rock game, which is a universal children's game in Japan, and used by adults where Westerners might toss a coin.

Yakyuu ken ("Baseball scissors-paper-rock"): A scissors-paper rock variant with chanting based on a baseball theme. If a geisha loses, she downs a cup of sake in one go. If a guest loses, he takes off a piece of clothing. These forfeits can be employed in the other games too. It's not unknown for older gentlemen to fling off their toupees when faced with the final catastrophe.

Edo de gozaimasu ("This is Edo"): A game

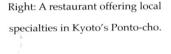
Right: A restaurant offering local specialties in Kyoto's Ponto-cho.

played in pairs, where Edo = samurai, Kyoto = nobleman, and Osaka = merchant. A: *This is Edo*. B (in samurai pose): *This is Kyoto*. A (in nobleman's pose): *This is Osaka*. B (in merchant's pose): *This is Edo* (or *Kyoto* or *Osaka*). A responds, and the game speeds up. The object is to rush the other player into mismatching the phrase and the pose, with the usual penalties accruing. The "samurai" pose is hand on hip; the nobleman's pose, hand on hand at chest level to mime holding a wooden sceptre; and the merchant's pose is a deep, commercial bow.

I-ro-ha no i no ji ("The 'A' in 'ABC'"): One for later in the evening, to a chant of (roughly), "How do you write your ABC, how do you write your A? This is how, this is how, how you write your A." The player/victim, facing out from the wall, uses their bottom to mime writing the letter. The Japanese chant, of course, does not feature the Roman alphabet. Instead it uses the traditional *i-ro-ha* syllabic script, derived from an ancient Buddhist poem on the vanity of worldly pleasures, which skillfully uses each letter just once. The first letter, *i*, consists of two graceful semicircular swoops, down, up, and down again.

The above game illustrates some of the difficulties uninitiated observers have in wrapping their minds around the flower-and-willow world. Japanese culture is by no means alone in mixing high art with broad humor, but is unusually exuberant in doing so. Western guests at geisha parties often misunderstand the whole thing. Faced with non-Japanese speakers in need of entertainment, geisha tend, if anything, to step up the fun-and-games side

of things. They know that their foreign guests' range of vision cannot possibly pick up the infra-reds and ultra-violets of what is happening around them. The men especially may expect something like a brothel, or they may expect everyone to be solemn. The flower-and-willow world is not a brothel, and it has never confused seriousness with solemnity. It cannot afford to; it would not exist unless the guests enjoyed themselves immensely. They do so

Above: The entrance curtain (*noren*) to a teahouse in Gion. Japanese heraldry is a stark, monochrome affair, and another proof of just how talented the culture is in graphic design.

partly because they can be as aesthetic or as childish as they wish. This is the flower-and-willow world; they are free. Until, that is, it all has to be paid for.

Which is why geisha accompany their clients down the corridors to the bathroom and wait outside the door. If a man gets time to himself, the reasoning goes, he may start to pine for his home, wife, and children. He may start to ruminate on just how much the evening is going to cost him. He may return to the *ozashiki* and ruin the atmosphere with his forebodings. So the geisha gaily chats to him through the door, talking about everything and nothing. She may even sing, if time permits. These trips in pairs are favorite times for proposals, decent and otherwise; it is not unknown for secret relationships to start under these less than ideally romantic circumstances.

On the very rare occasions *taikomochi* make an appearance, things can get quite raucous indeed. Their stories are usually highly erotic, and their dances match up. They may mime intercourse, gay or straight, and do dances with the geisha, holding the women's *obi* and corkscrewing around the room to imitate the traditional way of undressing them. A favorite skit involves playing three old ladies of increasing seniority, reminiscing on the time they lost their virginity—with nostalgia increasing with age. Their performances are mini-masterpieces of traditional theater, with very strong influences from the kabuki stage.

At the *ozashiki,* the *taikomochi* is in fact on the horns of an exquisite dilemma. His job is to liven up the party for both geisha and guests. However, the sight of the geisha enjoying the *taikomochi*'s ribaldry may make the male guests

Right: A geisha entertaining businessmen. For Japanese viewers, the photograph will immediately evoke the word *settai*—political/business elite wining and dining.

feel jealous or dull by comparison. The *taiko-mochi* works very carefully to avoid spoiling the festive mood. He keeps his stories and dances short, and gets the guests on their feet dancing themselves as quickly as possible. He will at least pretend to enjoy their efforts, however atrocious. His hair is cropped short, to emphasize his lack of sensual appeal. It helps that *taikomochi* are at least middle-aged. The terms of their employment forbid relationships with geisha, but they are only human—although supernaturally so, if some of their stories are to be believed.

An *ozashiki* party usually lasts for two hours, sometimes three. Some *ozashiki* may be very different from the outline given above. Some guests are so dull that all efforts to get them to enjoy themselves fail, and the evening declines into a few rounds of dancing and desultory chat. In other cases, the guests are there not just for fun, but primarily to use the *ochaya* as a prestigious and secure venue for negotiations. This is especially common in the Tokyo districts of Akasaka and Shimbashi, which are favorite haunts of the capital's political and business elites. The clientele is well heeled in every major hanamachi, even the relatively popular Asakusa. Geisha may serve drinks and talk briefly with guests in these circumstances, but they are chiefly valued for staying in the background and divulging nothing of what they hear.

Before returning home for the night, geisha may go to dinner with guests or their *danna* if they have one. This is part of their work, and the men they dine with will be billed for their

time, just as if they were being entertained at an *ozashiki*. In days long gone by, Kyoto geisha used to party for free with the students of Kyoto University at the end of the day. Many love affairs formed. The young men were

Above: A teahouse in Gion. The windows are hung with *yoshizu* reed screens, to protect guests from the prying eyes of the outside world.

assured of top positions later, so they were valued for their networking potential. These days, some geisha do a stint at the so-called "home bar" which many *ochaya* operate. These are tiny lounges within the building, with a counter and a few tables. A known face can drop in for a quiet drink and perhaps a chat with a maiko or geiko. He will not bankrupt himself in the process—the bill may come to only the price of a meal at a very exclusive French restaurant. A giveaway, by hanamachi standards.

Paying for an *ozashiki* party is not for the faint-hearted. The costs are so phenomenal that very few guests can afford to pay out of their own money. Expense accounts are the norm. The bill is called *hana-dai* ("flower charge"). Asakusa also uses the word *tamagushi*, meaning an offering of a sacred sprig to a Shinto god. For billing purposes, geisha's time is calculated

in units called *sticks*. Before clocks were common, the geisha kept track of the passage of time by how many sticks of incense had been used up. (To this day, clocks are not hung in *ochaya*). Each hanamachi used different lengths, so the value of one stick varies from five to thirty minutes depending on the district. On top the geisha fees, there is a charge for the use of the *ochaya*, which includes paying the large specialist staff, and in addition the caterer's bill and charges for drinks.

Except for the very generous tips which guests offer to the geisha in special envelopes, no money changes hands on the night itself. The comedown would be much too sobering for the guests. Hanamachi insiders are disgusted when businessmen ask for receipts to present to their companies. The flower-and-willow world works on trust. Fussing over details and

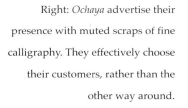

Right: *Ochaya* advertise their presence with muted scraps of fine calligraphy. They effectively choose their customers, rather than the other way around.

brandishing pieces of paper is the basest form of bad manners.

Bills are routed through the *kemban*, the hanamachi's auditing and registration office. Each morning, the audit officers collect slips from the *ochaya*, which detail the total cost of the previous night's parties. The *kemban* then cross-checks the *ochaya*'s total geisha fees with the various *okiya* which have supplied performers to the party. Once they are passed, the *ochaya* is free to bill the guest, which is normally done directly to his company or home once a month. In the very rare event that payment is not forthcoming, the *ochaya* simply turns to the man who introduced the guest in the first place. He is the culprit's senior, and the hanamachi is a closed circle, so he is expected to take responsibility for the matter. The consequences for his reputation if he did not would be unimagin-

able. He is already in hot water for having introduced a rogue customer. The *ochaya* pays the caterers and sends the remainder to the local geisha union, which gives a cut to the *kemban* for administrative costs, before forwarding the balance to the *okiya* as payment for the performers.

Actual amounts vary enormously, depending on the length of the party, the number of guests, the number of geisha and trainees, and so on. A geisha's basic fee is never under 10,000 Yen an hour. A month's to two months' pay for a salaried worker would be a conservative baseline to start from. In practice, the full total may come to a number of multiples of that if the party has been especially lavish or the guests exceptionally well off. Estimated ability to pay is one factor in the *ochaya*'s calculation of the bill. The basic rule for guests goes without

Left: A dance performance at a small-scale, intimate party.

saying: if you even suspect you can't afford it, then you definitely can't—and you will not be given the chance to prove it. Protecting people from the delusion that they can pay is one function of the "no new faces" rule; the *ochaya* effectively choose their customers, and not the other way around.

Other Parties and Promotional Events

The pattern of rehearsal, research, and *ozashiki* performance is the fundamental rhythm of hanamachi life, but it is not the only one. Performances in hotels, catering to dozens of guests, are quite common. There are large-scale one-off shows too for the Friends of the *Ookini*

Right: A dancer performs the Ponto-cho Odori at the Ponto-cho Kaburenjo Theater in Kyoto. Public dances like these evolved from the late nineteenth century onward.

Zaidan, an officially sponsored support organization for the Kyoto geisha districts. Likewise, other hanamachi sometimes arrange one-offs for large groups, in order to get more people—especially students—interested in hanamachi culture. Individual geisha may also give *Nihon buyo* and shamisen performances. Some find it a lucrative sideline.

Maiko are in especially heavy demand nationwide because they exist in Kyoto only, and exert such a strong grip on the whole image of the flower-and-willow world. They travel quite a lot to other cities for publicity shots, kimono shows, and the like. And like the great characters of the nineteenth and early twentieth centuries, they occasionally travel abroad. More than anything else, however, the break in the daily routine is provided by the annual calendar of events, both intimate hanamachi events and the vast public events which have evolved since the late nineteenth century. We will finish this chapter with an overview of them. But before that, we will look at the very last day of a geisha's career—retirement.

Retirement: *Hiki-iwai*

The ceremony to mark a geisha's retirement is called *hiki-iwai*, literally "the celebration of being pulled"—pulled out, that is, of the hanamachi. In the days when every geisha had a *danna*, this meant that he paid off all her outstanding debts and set her up as a mistress. It is now, of course, a voluntary act on the part of the performer. Many leave to get married. Others open their own businesses, especially

small bars or restaurants. Every large city in Japan has at least a few such places, where customers can enjoy something of the flavor of the flower-and-willow world at a fraction of the cost. Aficionados of *Nihon buyo* and shamisen also gather there. The geisha profession is not the only one to follow this pattern. Most towns also have restaurants and bars run by retired sumo wrestlers, who reminisce on their glory days over large fortifying bowls of *chanko-nabe*

stew, the food which helps to build up the wrestlers' bulk.

The *hiki-iwai* ceremony is one of the simplest. Retiring geisha hand out boxes of cooked rice to ex-colleagues and teachers. Sometimes, a little red rice is mixed in, to convey the geisha's mixed feelings about retirement. White rice and domesticity is all very well, but the day may come when she wishes to return to the color and excitement of the flower-and-willow world.

Above: Under a celebratory red and white canopy, a poster advertises the Cherry Dances. Flanking it are sales prices for bolts of *obi* cloth and other fabrics. This is a good example of the interdependence of the flower-and-willow world and the crafts and professions that surround it.

Above right: Heron dancers parade in the Gion Festival in Kyoto.

Below right: A historical character in the Festival of the Ages (*Jidai Matsuri*) parade, Kyoto.

Festivals and Seasonal Events
Kyoto

The Kyoto calendar is especially elaborate. The following list is not exhaustive and covers only some of the highlights.

Commencement ceremony (January 7, Gion Kobu): Maiko and geiko assemble at the Yasaka Nyokobo Academy and promise to do all they can to improve their performance skills during the coming year. Formal vows like this are a common feature of Japanese life. Athletes, for example, proclaim their determination to give their all at the opening of school sports days and other tournaments.

Setsubun (February 2–4): All Japanese families celebrate this festival by throwing beans out the window, to keep evil spirits outside (*soto*) and invite good fortune inside (*uchi*). The hana-

machi celebrate by dressing up and entertaining in bizarre costumes—over-the-top Chinese costumes, TV personalities, and so on. There is an element of carnival in the proceedings. Customers may cross-dress, and a lot of alcohol is consumed by all and sundry.

Oishi Kuranosuke Commemoration (March 20): The Head of the Inoue School dances at the Ichirikitei *ochaya*, in honor of the hero of the samurai epic *Chuushingura* or "The Tale of the Forty-Seven Masterless Samurai." (The title literally means "A Storehouse of Faithful Retainers"). Just like Clint Eastwood's spaghetti westerns capture something fundamental in the American psyche, this true tale of gory revenge shows a portrait of the samurai as he is meant to be.

Left: An ornate float is drawn
through the streets during the
Gion Festival.

A naïve provincial lord, Lord Asano, was
appointed to oversee protocol for ceremonies
before the shogun, and he turned for advice on
etiquette to the great courtier Lord Kira. Lord
Asano was no man of *tsu*, and failed to give
Lord Kira the appropriate lavish gifts. The
aggrieved courtier therefore selected an entirely
inappropriate costume for Asano's first
ceremony. The shamed and insulted lord
drew his sword on the spot, and slightly
wounded Kira. It was justifiable, but not in the
shogun's palace; the hapless Lord Asano was
commanded to commit *seppuku*—ritual self-
disembowelment.

It could all have been averted if Asano's
trusted veteran retainer, Oishi Kuranosuke, had
been there. In Edo, many awaited his arrival
from the provinces; he was sure to avenge his
lord. He did no such thing. In fact, the now
masterless samurai launched himself into a
career of debauchery which scandalized the
people of the time (it was 1703). He lay drunk
in the streets, his sword rusted in its scabbard,
and proclaimed self-gratification the highest
aim in life. His former friends cursed and spat
on him, but he seemed (and often was) oblivi-
ous. The nadir came in Kyoto, where he was
spotted drunkenly stumbling around the
Ichirikitei, playing blind-man's-buff with a
group of giggling maids. He was the epitome of
a "dog samurai"—a man beyond shame.

It was all an elaborate ruse, of course. On a
snowy December night, Oishi and a trusted
group of forty-seven comrades attacked Lord
Kira's palace. They had done whatever it took
to throw Kira off their scent and keep up the

*He was the epitome of a
"dog samurai"—a man
beyond shame.*

Right: Wearing brightly colored
kimonos, geisha file onstage to
perform the Cherry Dances at the
Gion Kaburenjo theater.

vendetta. Some had divorced their wives, others had sold them; one man had to kill his father-in-law. It worked; the attack was a complete surprise. The dastardly Lord Kira was found cowering in an outhouse. He was recognized and promptly parted from his head. The masterless samurai paraded it to Asano's grave, applauded by all Edo. The shogun was so impressed with their virtue that he did not execute them as common criminals. They were allowed the honorable death of *seppuku*, and their gravesite in Tokyo is even now a place of pilgrimage. It is this connection with the *Chuushingura* epic that makes the Ichirikitei Kyoto's most prestigious *ochaya*.

The Cherry Dances (April): Known in Japanese as the *Miyako odori*, this is Gion Kobu's premier public performance, and lasts through the month at the *kaburenjo*. It has eight dance pieces, with kabuki/*bunraku*-derived themes, all with a seasonal flavor. The story of Minamoto Yoshitsune is among those enacted.

Kyo-odori and Kitano-odori (April): Miyagawa-cho's and Kami Shichiken's annual

Below: Four geisha play musical instruments—*kotsuzumi* drums and flute—as part of the Cherry Dances.

dance performances respectively. The *Kyo-odori* festival features traditional folk songs and, like the hanamachi itself, has a strong local following.

Kamogawa-odori (May): Ponto-cho's annual dance performance.

Dances of the Six Districts (June): A two-day event held at Kyoto Kaikan Hall, involving dances from all five Kyoto geisha districts (the sixth, Shimabara, is no longer an active hanamachi). The grand finale features a dance performed by the combined maiko.

Gion Festival (July 1–31): A major spectacular, climaxing on July 17, when massive traditional floats topped with soaring poles are wheeled through the streets, looking for all the world like something out of Tolkien. Maiko and geiko perform as part of the festival on July 17.

Kami Shichiken Beer Garden (July 1–August 31): Outdoor "beer gardens" loosely based on the Bavarian style are popular events during the summer. Kami Shichiken's beer garden is an informal event held at the local *kaburenjo*. It is open to all comers, and is a great

Below: Dance performances at local *kaburenjo* (geisha theaters) are accessible to the general public.

Above: A light kimono called *yukata* is commonly worn during the summer, especially during festivals, as on this ornate float rolling through Kyoto during the Gion Festival.

Kaomise (December): The flower-and-willow world reviews the next year's cast of kabuki actors, as they present themselves to the public at the Minami-za Theatre. The geiko and maiko go all-out to be the most splendid of them all.

Flame Ceremony (December 31): In this beautiful event, people visit the Yasaka Shrine in Gion and receive a sacred flame, which they take home to light their cooking fires for the New Year. Some maiko and geiko are among those who take straw torches to the shrine to be lit.

Tokyo

The Tokyo calendar contains far fewer spectacular public events than Kyoto's. The largest and best known is the Shimbashi district's *Azuma Odori* ("Dances of the East"), held from May 28–May 31, at the Shimbashi Theatre, which is located in the Ginza district. Even this premier event is a much scaled-down survivor. It used to last a whole month, like the Cherry Dances in Kyoto. It differs from Miyagawa-cho's *Kyo-odori* too, in that it does not attract a strong local following. Tokyo has changed vastly more than Kyoto in the post-war period, and relatively few urban localities retain strong links with their past. A partial exception is the Asakusa district, which offers the following events:

Year Opening Festival (January 5): Dance in formal black kimonos.

Setsubun (early February): Dance in zany costumes, similar to Kyoto Setsubun.

opportunity to mix informally with the maiko and geiko, who dress quite informally themselves.

Festival of the Ages (October 22): An elaborate parade of people in costumes representing the various eras of Japanese history, starting with the Heian period. Gion and Ponto-cho geisha take turns each year to play the famous beauties of each age. Ono no Komachi, Murasaki Shikibu, and Shizuka Gozen are among the turnout. The parade finishes at the Heian Shrine.

Gion-odori (November): This is the annual performance of Gion Higashi, the smaller of the Gion hanamachi.

Birthday of Kannon, Goddess of Mercy (March 18): "Dance of the Golden Dragon."

Three Shrines Festival (Mid-May): Group dancing by geisha from various hanamachi, featuring *taikomochi* performance.

Kanda Festival (Mid-May): At Kanda Myojin Shrine. One of Tokyo's three largest festivals. Features dance performance by geisha.

Teragiku Memorial Dance (October 18): featuring "Dance of the Golden Dragon."

Tokyo Festival of the Ages (November 3): featuring geisha from various hanamachi.

These events are publicized by the *Asakusa geisha to o-tanoshimi kai* ("Society for Having Fun with the Asakusa Geisha"). Paradoxically, Tokyo offers at least as many chances as Kyoto for ordinary people to see something of the geisha world. Some of the options are explored in Appendix I.

Above left: A member of the parade in the *Jidai Matsuri* (Festival of the Ages).

Below left: A geisha is carried through town during Osaka's Yebisu Festival. Yebisu is a Chinese deity, one of the Seven Lucky Gods who brings good fortune in business. Situated close to Kyoto, Osaka has a vibrant, irreverent mercantile culture. The city is the capital of Japanese comedy.

CHAPTER 5

geisha dress

A geisha's costume includes a stunning array of sumptuous fabrics and precious materials.

烏居清満画

Grav. impr. par GILLOT

Right: A courtesan wearing a silk kimono and *obi* with wooden sandals and a broad-brimmed hat. All the elements of geisha dress were adopted from the fashions of the mid-eighteenth century. Note the disc-shaped family crest (*mon*) near the shoulder.

Far right: The geisha's white make-up marks her off as belonging to the flower-and-willow world. It makes the wearer a powerful symbol of her art.

pongee, *ro* and *sha*. This is for the costumes alone; the accessories require a variety of separate grades of handmade paper, boxwood for combs, and paper, silk, and bamboo for parasols, fans, and handbags. For mature geisha, human hair (usually imported) is needed for wigs—and the makeup itself has historically pressed some quite surprising substances into service.

Though the elements of the geisha look are truly extravagant, they were all drawn from fashions that commonly existed in the past. Before Japan was reluctantly opened up to the world, all Japanese women wore hairpins, kimonos, and *obi*. The geisha never belonged to a separate, caged world like the *tayu* and *oiran* courtesans did. What the flower-and-willow world did was to take pre-existing elements and push them to an extreme of sophistication.

Kimonos

Geisha value kimonos over all other possessions, and refer to them as their "souls" and the indispensable badge of their craft. Japanese culture prizes uniforms of all sorts, and it is easy to understand how special their costumes are to geisha. Displayed on a stand, a kimono is a truly spectacular sight. What strikes the eye even before the sumptuousness of the fabric and the beauty of the designs is the sheer volume of the material. A standard kimono is made of a unit of cloth called a *tan*—a strip twelve metres long and thirty-seven centimeters wide. Kimonos for maiko and geiko take twice that amount. In the depths of winter,

Right: A maiko in full attire. When walking on the street, geisha hold their kimono hems with the left hand. In the past, this was another way of indicating that they were not courtesans.

The flower-and-willow world has never believed in stinting. A geisha's costume includes a stunning array of sumptuous fabrics and precious materials. At any one time, the ensemble will include most or all of the following: figured satin, silk damask, brocades, gold leaf, gold thread, silver, silver thread, jade, coral, tortoiseshell, diamond, amethyst, agate, paulownia wood (for footwear), and fabrics almost unknown in the West, such as

three *tan* of material are used. A garment of this type may weigh twenty kilos (or roughly half a maiko). Learning to bear the weight nonchalantly is all part of the job.

The Kyoto geisha districts are the only remaining communities where Japanese dress is worn all day every day by almost everyone involved. Modern Japan has almost abandoned kimonos, reserving it for rites of passage like weddings and coming of age ceremonies. While many women still love kimonos, most find them too constricting to wear every day. Also, putting them on is a skill which has to be learned, and the skill has died out in most families. Kimonos have no buttons and all come in the same size. The wearer wraps the robe around herself, tucks it together left over right (superstition forbids otherwise), and fastens it

Above left: As the maiko's career progresses, her red collar (*eri*) becomes gradually appliquéd over in silver. Here, we can see the appliqué edging down the collar toward the shoulder blades. When the two sides meet, it will be time for *erikae*—changing the collar and becoming a geiko.

Below left: Geisha poring over bolts of brightly-patterned cloth at a festival.

at the front with braids, a dozen of them in all. Then comes the most difficult part of the operation—tying the *obi*. It requires physical strength as well as dexterity, which is why many geisha have assistant dressers.

The hanamachi revolves around kimonos. Having them designed, selecting them to wear, receiving them as gifts, and passing them on to younger geisha are all parts of everyday life. Since geisha wear their kimonos every day, they do not fasten them quite as tightly as the average Japanese woman. They are worn looser, and hang down to reveal the nape. These days, many people are no longer used to wearing kimonos, and feel uncomfortable in them. They also *look* uncomfortable. Part of the charm of geisha is that they look like they really belong in them.

In the modern world, many women wear off-the-peg kimonos, with pre-tied *obi*. They are sometimes made of artificial fibers for ease of washing. One prefers not to imagine what would happen to such garments in the hanamachi, though a picture of a *shikomi* scrubbing a floor does spring to mind. It goes without saying that all kimonos in the flower-and-willow world are handmade in silk. They are one-of-kind tailor-made garments which can easily cost a typical year's salary and more.

Along with the *obi* and other accessories, kimonos send out clear signals about the wearer's status in the geisha district. This is of course especially true of Kyoto. Maiko kimonos are similar in principle to all traditional garments for younger women. They emphasize the wearer's youth and beauty, and the fact that she is single. Her unmarried status is proclaimed by the wide sleeves. Maikos' are extravagant, hanging down past the knee. (Shades of the Heian noblewomen, with their sleeves trailing from the windows of their carriages. Fluttering the sleeves were, in the past, a declaration of love). The kimono is worn long, trailing over the floor at *ozashiki*, and held up by the hem with one hand when walking off-tatami.

Junior maikos' kimonos are richly patterned with motifs which reflect the season—chrysanthemums, water patterns, maple leaves, autumn grasses, turtles and cranes, and a host of other seasonal markers (we will look at some of them in more detail through hairpins). The higher the rank, the more restrained the designs become. Senior maiko wear slightly less patterned kimonos, with one shoulder not decorated. Geiko's costumes do not feature decorative motifs above the *obi*. The sleeves are narrower, and after three years the train is not allowed to sweep along the ground. By the time they are in their forties, geisha kimonos are relatively *jimi*—restrained and subdued—relative to younger geisha, that is. On formal occasions, for debuts and so on, both maiko and geiko wear black kimonos marked with five crests on the back, sleeves, and front. They can also wear colored plain-patterned crested kimonos to semi-formal events. Independent *jimae* geiko wear their personal family crests, while maiko and geiko living in *okiya* wear the crest of their geisha house. Even formal black kimonos feature sumptuous designs if intended for maiko.

Japan is hot in the summer, and crushingly humid. Most areas have snowfalls in the winter.

The hanamachi revolves around kimonos.

Left: Japanese *Tsuzure-ori* weaving allows a weaver to make a finely detailed scenes from a painted design. A finished *obi*, the kimono sash, can take up to a year to weave and can sell for $10,000 or more.

Kyoto in particular bakes and freezes its inhabitants through the year, because it lies in a low area flanked by mountains. Kimonos have to reflect the passing seasons not just through patterns, but in their materials as well. August temperatures reach 35 degrees Celsius and over. Kimonos made from silk gauze materials like *ro* and *sha* (a slightly coarser gauze) are worn during the late summer.

A boldly-patterned unlined cotton robe called a *yukata* is worn in informal situations, indoors and out. Spring and autumn kimonos are lined and of heavier silk, and winter garments are double-lined and padded at the bottom.

Fabrics

Traditional Japanese clothing uses a wide variety of fabrics. In the past, hemp, ramie (made from a common weed similar to hemp), and silk were the most widely used. Almost all farmhouses contained a loom, and sericulture was an important secondary source of income for most families. However, sumptuary laws prohibited ordinary people from wearing fine silk. Fine silk consists of thread teased from the silkworm cocoon and reeled. They were allowed to wear pongee, a fabric made from silk floss, which is spun in the same way as cotton or wool. Fine silk was a prerogative of the samurai and nobles, though merchants

Right: These maiko are dressed for April, the cherry blossom viewing season.

continually broke the sumptuary laws, and there was no question of the geisha wearing anything less, legal or not. Ironically, pongee today is one of Japan's rarest and most sought after fabrics. [39]

Weaves and Weavers

Japanese silk is worked up into a wide variety of weaves—plain and figured twills and satins, damasks, *ro* and *sha* gauzes, and plain fabrics.

The powerhouse of silk weaving in Kyoto (and indeed in the whole country) is an area called Nishijin, near the Kami Shichiken geisha district. Its silks are the most highly prized in Japan, and the elite of the weaving hierarchy has traditionally formed the core of the nearby hanamachi's clientele. They are referred to as Father by the geiko and maiko. This is a special term of respect for them. Even the name of the weaving district is steeped in Kyoto history. Nishijin means "west camp"—the military headquarters of one of the sides fighting the Onin War in the fifteenth century, which razed Kyoto to the ground. Like flower arranging, the craft of weaving somehow survived the chaos and flourished. The area's dyed yarn is woven into kimonos, *obi,* and tapestries by a workforce numbering in the thousands. Their product is in great demand nationwide and is produced sparingly.

Dyeing and Other Methods of Patterning

Kimono fabrics can be patterned by weaving the design into the cloth using different colored threads or by applying dyes to the finished cloth itself. Kimonos are dyed using a number of processes—vat dyeing, shaped resist or tie-dying, painting, and stenciling. Geisha kimonos also feature embroidery using applied metallic leaf.

The most celebrated of Japanese methods is called *kyo-yuzen*. The technique employs only handmade dyes derived from natural sources like tree bark and berries. The expense of the process is compounded by the application of patterns. Designs are handpainted onto the cloth, in minute profusion, by skilled artisans. The treasured result is used in maiko and geiko's formal kimonos. In summer, freshly dyed *Kyo-yuzen* cloth is washed in the waters of the River Kamo, which flows through central Kyoto.

Tailoring a kimono calls for very fine accuracy, but it can be done very quickly. The finished material is cut into eight panels and finely stitched together. An expert tailor can work up a kimono in a single day or less, and the garments can be disassembled with equal ease for cleaning or repair. Apart from the intrinsic cost of the fabrics, the real expense comes from the preparation of the cloth itself.

The Collar

Mention has been made before of the collar (*eri*) as a symbol of seniority among geisha. The collar is a detachable strip of cloth sewn at the back of the kimono neck. Maiko's are red, and progressively appliqued with silver thread. The "changing of the collar" (*erikae*) from red to white marks the transition from maiko to geiko.

Designs are handpainted onto the cloth, in minute profusion, by skilled artisans.

Obi and *Obi* Accessories

The essential job of the *obi* is to hold the kimono shut and up to a few centuries ago nothing more was made of it. (In much the same way that the essential job of Venice was to house Venetians). *Obi* are now crafted usually in brocade, and each one is designed with a specific kimono in mind. They are as much works of art as the kimono itself, and tying them in beautiful knots is an indispensable skill for kimono aficionados. They are held in place with anything up to fifteen bands and fasteners, again of silk, brocade, and precious metals and stones.

Obi is usually rendered into English as "sash" or "cummerbund," which is even more unsatisfactory. A standard *obi* is a strip of cloth

about four meters long and thirty centimeters wide. It is tied tightly around the waist and up over the lower ribcage. A maiko's *obi* is a meter longer, gorgeously decorated with gold and silver threads, and tied so that it hangs down at the back almost to her ankles. A geiko's is of the standard length and width, and usually fastened in a neat boxy knot.

The geisha fashion of tying the *obi* at the back, as opposed to the front, was a very significant fashion statement in the past. It sharply distinguished them from the *tayu*, *oiran*, and other courtesans, who tied theirs at the front to proclaim their sexual availability to the highest acceptable bidder. The geisha *obi* is thus a symbol of the dignity of the craft and shows their distinction from the courtesans of the past.

Obi Accessories

There are three main accessories for the *obi*—the *obi-jime* (*obi* braid), *obi-dome* or *pocchiri* (*obi* clasp), and *obi-age* (*obi* support). Together they build up an extravagant, multi-layered look for the *obi*, proclaiming the money and craft that have been put into the artist who wears them. This is of course especially true of the maiko look; geisha tone things down in all aspects of their costume.

The *obi-age* is a narrow strip of silk cloth and its role is to help support the *obi*. Maiko *obi-age* are highly ornate and the red cloth is decorated with both gold and silver embroidery. They are worn to be visible above the *obi*. The *obi-age* that geiko wear are less ornate, and so are worn inside the *obi*.

Right: Three Boat Festival (*Mifune Matsuri*), Kyoto. If one compares this photograph with the ordinary ladies' kimono on page 11, one can see just how outrageously revealing the back of the maiko's *hikizure* kimono is.

Left: Two maiko in kimonos and *obi* walk side-by-side on a Kyoto street. The crest of their *okiya* is embroidered at the bottom of their *obi*. Like their kimonos, their *obi* are handmade for one specific person to wear.

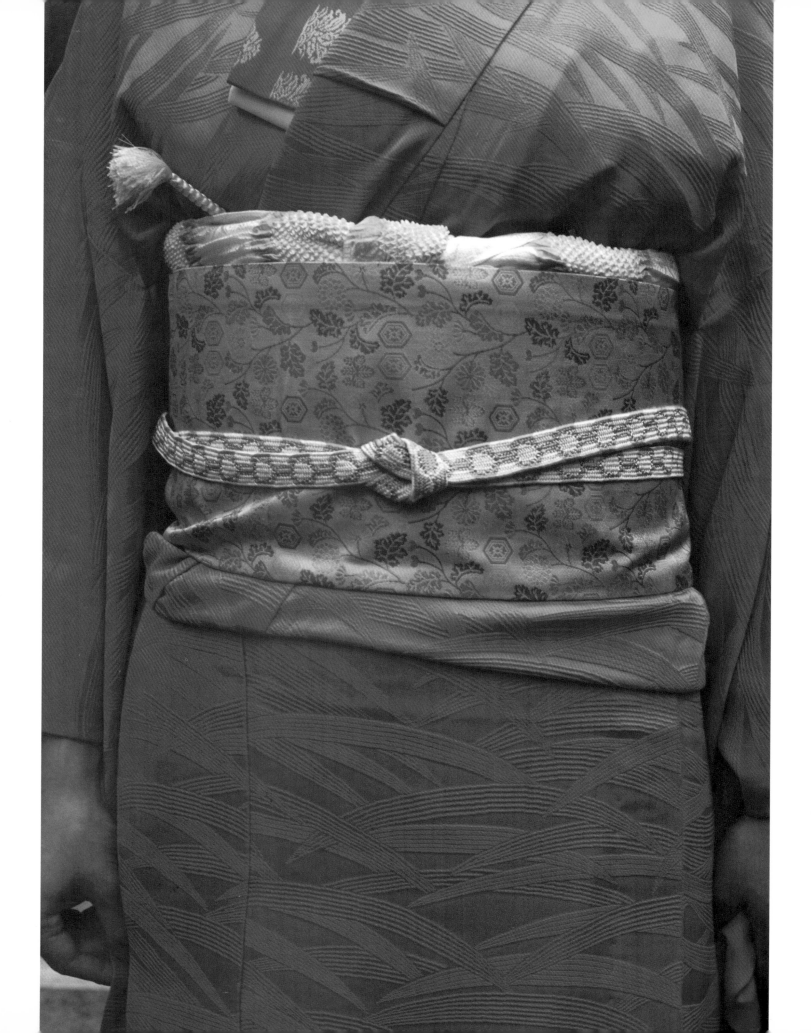

Far left: The *obi* is a symbol of the dignity of the geisha craft. The outermost layer is the narrow *obi-jime* braid, which is fastened around the floral-patterned *obi* proper. Underneath that comes the *obi-age* (*obi* support). The wearer is a fully-qualified geiko, and thus does not wear the elaborate *pocchiri* (*obi* clasp), which adorns the maiko's *obi* braid.

Left: A geisha wears the delicate, formal headdress and kimono prescribed by tradition. Geishas' hair ornaments and the patterns on their kimono and *obi* usually reflect the season. This is the standard maiko *wareshinobu* hairstyle.

The *obi-jime*, or braid, is a narrow band of stippled silk thread encircling the waist, holding the whole construction together. The braid is horizontally striped and comes in very bright color combinations indeed such as sky blue and white, scarlet, and silver lamé, even a custard yellow with peppermint green. Because they are so narrow against the *obi* itself they work surprisingly well, adding a subtle punctuation to the riot of red, silver, and gold that is the maiko midriff.

The maiko's *obi* clasp is a spectacular and very costly piece of sculpture. The frame is made of silver and mounted with coral, jade, agate, diamonds, and other precious stones. Geiko forgo the precious stones. They often forgo the *obi* clasp itself. "The plainer the more powerful" is the rule, after all, in the flower-and-willow world.

Hair Ornaments and Hairstyle
Hairpins

The maiko's ornamented hairpins, or *kanzashi*, are one of the visual glories of the profession. They are usually composed of two parts, a miniature bouquet, with half a dozen streamers hanging down. They trace a cycle through the seasons of the Japanese year, and many of the symbols they employ are echoed in kimono fabrics and other decorations. These symbols are also generally used in Japanese society. No other culture appreciates the seasons more.

January: This hairpin varies from year to year, always using motifs connected with the festival. Traditional New Year pastimes include

flying kites and spinning tops, so these may be included.

February: This month sees the first flower-viewing event of the year. The plum blossom is cherished in Japan second only to the cherry blossom. Plum trees are planted in gardens and beauty spots all over Japan, and bonsai plum trees in blossom are exhibited indoors, each with a placard on which a haiku is written. The maiko hairpin features plum blossom, or alternatively daffodils.

March: With its warm golden color and more fortunate Japanese name, the rape plant is thought of as a herald of spring.

April: This month's hairpin features cherry blossom, one of the culture's major obsessions. TV news bulletins broadcast live from the Cherry Front Line as the wave of pink sweeps northward over the country. The most romantic scenes of the most romantic movies take place in what is known as a "snowstorm of cherry blossoms." Every patch of cherry trees in the

Above: Rice panicles, worn in a maiko's hair, are thought to bring good luck for a prosperous New Year.

Far left: A maiko with the ambiguous expression known in Japan as an "archaic smile" (from classical sculpture). Lips are drawn in smaller than they are, to create the ideal rosebud shape.

country is underlayed with a carpet of revelers in varying and sometimes extreme states of disrepair. A butterfly hairpin is also worn at this time of year.

May: The motif of the month is wisteria and iris.

June: June is a humid, rainy month over most of the country. Hairpins of willow or hydrangea do a little to impart a less dank tone to proceedings in the flower-and-willow world.

July: This is the month of the Gion Festival, one of the three largest festivals in Japan. A different hairpin is designed each year for the occasion, and Kyoto habitues keenly look forward to it. The month's other motif is a fan—not a semicircular dancing fan but an oval one that is used to stir the sultry air in search of some coolness.

August: The morning glory, with its long Kyoto connections through the tea master Sen no Rikyu among others, is the symbol of the month. Japanese pampas grass is also used.

September: The Chinese bell flower motif is arranged in elegant violet and white streams as a symbol of the beginning of autumn.

October: The chrysanthemum is both the symbol of October and the crest of the imperial family. It also adorns the Japanese passport.

November: Japan's autumn foliage is as spectacular as Canada's, and trips into the mountains to view the splendid scenery are popular. The seasonal hairpin features a russet maple leaf.

December: Round, white rice cakes are a feature of the Japanese New Year, and the December hairpin is composed of white flowers which resemble them. This is the hairpin autographed by kabuki stars at their annual *kaomise* debut; there are two miniscule sign-boards at the bottom of the streamer especially for the purpose.

Hairstyles

There are five maiko hairsytyles:

Wareshinobu: As already discussed, this is the maiko's first hairstyle. The hair is first dressed with a preparation called *bintsuke-abura,* which helps fix the styling. Apart from the red-and-white spotted ribbon and seasonal hairpin, the hair is held in place with a decorated horizontal pin through the back of the bun. A further pin hods the bun from the top, and flutters are affixed above the right temple to a second red ribbon arching over the head.

Ofuku: A simplified version of the *wareshinobu,* with only one red ribbon, visible at the back of the head. This was the hairstyle which proclaimed the end of the maiko's virginity. It now informs the viewer of her graduation to senior maiko status.

Katsuyama and yakko-shimada: Two formal styles, the former for the Gion Festival and the latter for the New Year period.

Sakko: Worn for the last month of a maiko's career. Cutting the hair partly or shaving it off altogether are sometimes signs of resolution in Japanese culture. The cropping of the top of the bun for this style is read as a symbol of the maiko's resolve to take the plunge and become a geiko.

Geiko wigs

The wig is another handcrafted and highly expensive (about 500,000 Yen) element of the geiko's wardrobe. A geiko requires three of them in separate styles. The *shimada* style is worn to formal events; the *tsubushi-shimada* is

Far left: This flamboyant style harks back to the complex coiffure of the *tayu* courtesans of Kyoto.

Below: A shop selling *kushi* and *kanzashi,* Japanese hair ornaments.

Right: Geisha wigs, in the *tsubushi-shimada* style, and the *shimada* style for more formal events.

more commonly but by no means always worn. The *mae-ware* style is worn only during dance performances, and only when the dancer is playing a male role. In general, wigs are worn only for the first few years of a geiko's career, as is the white makeup. In later years, however, both may be worn from time to time when required for certain dance performances.

Geiko also forgo the maiko's elaborate roster of *kanzashi* hairpins. In summer they wear jade hairpins and in winter coral. Combs are of silver and tortoiseshell respectively. In olden times, Japanese women used long hairpins for self-defence when called upon to do so, and maiko are kept well aware of the tradition as part of their glamorous heritage. The former geisha Iwasaki Mineko relates another, unexpected defensive capability of the coral hairpin:

"It breaks apart when put in contact with poisoned liquids." [40] The legend shows something of the long history of the flower-and-willow world as a gathering place for politics.

Makeup

The history of white makeup goes back to the Heian period, when it was worn by nobles at imperial audiences in dark inner chambers. Traditionally, one of the ingredients was dried nightingale droppings, which were apparently valued as a tonic for the skin. Ingredients are now less exotic.

To ready the skin for the makeup, an oil-based paste is applied first. The white makeup is then brushed on from the neck down and nape down. A stencil is used for the maiko's unpainted "w" on the nape. For a number of

Left: Preparing for the evening. The robe is a light, informal *yukata*.

Above right: For special occasions such as the *omisedashi* (debut), three strips of flesh are left bare.

Below right: An unusual photograph of a performer putting on her makeup on a local train.

special occasions like the *omisedashi* debut three tines of unpainted flesh are left bare. Finally the face is made up and powdered, and eyeliner, eyebrow paint, and lipstick added. Getting the whole process right is the maiko's or geiko's own responsibility. This approach to makeup is widely shared in East Asian performance arts. In kabuki and Peking opera, the actors have to master much more complex makeup routines as part of their mental preparation for playing a character onstage.

Underwear

Western-style underwear tends to spoil the line of the kimono, so geisha often wear more traditional Japanese styles. The bust may be wrapped in a strip of bleached cotton popularly known as *sarashi*. Two underlayers are worn, called *hada-juban* and *naga-juban*. The *hada-juban* is a buttonless blouse-like garment, closed left over right like the kimono (one has to be dead to do it the other way around). The *naga-juban* is a very elegant garment, a full-length underkimono patterned with bold white floral designs. For maiko the background is red, and for geiko pink. The *naga-juban* closely follows the line of the kimono, down to the long trailing sleeves of the maiko's costume. One can sometimes glimpse the scarlet *naga-juban* under-sleeve, while she dances or perhaps pours sake, and many men consider the moment erotically charged. The hem of the *naga-juban* can also be seen hanging below that of the kimono. The tradition of sumptuous, visible undergarments goes back a long way in Japan. Merchants and other lower orders used

Left: A maiko taking a photograph. The red and white *naga-juban* is visible at her right kimono sleeve.

fine underclothes as a way to display their wealth, but stay inside (or close to) the letter of the law on who could wear what in public.

Footwear

Traditional Japan had a great wealth of footwear styles, reflecting status, occupation, and personal taste. Some regret the relative poverty of Western-style footwear, especially for men. The two main styles are *zori*, soft slippers worn by women, and *geta*, wooden sandals worn by both sexes. *Geta* are still worn quite commonly in warm weather, and the clonk-clonk sound they make on the street is considered the epitome of summer.

The maiko's street footwear, however, is one of a kind. The ten-centimeter tall *okobo* clogs,

Right: These soft sandals are known as *zori*. Along with cleated *tabi* socks, they are standard footwear for ladies' kimonos. *Tabi* are invariably white and hook up at the side.

Far right: A geisha picking out her footwear as she leaves a large gathering. In situations like this, an experienced geisha can perform a highly accurate census of the assembly as she arrives. The footwear is a store of information on gender, age, status, and even profession.

Below: Wooden *geta* clogs. These come in a multitude of shapes and styles. The ones pictured here belong to a traditional restaurant, and have seen considerable use.

made of paulownia wood, help add to the maiko's character as being apart. Geiko *geta* are also made of paulownia, much lower, but plat-formed with two blocks of wood like a Stonehenge arch. Like all of Japan, the flower-and-willow world sheds its shoes when it goes indoors, leaving them off at the entrance vestibule known as the *genkan*. Most Japanese buildings have this definite boundary between the outside (*soto*) and inside (*uchi*); it is written with characters meaning "occult (or dark) barrier."

Both maiko and geiko wear white buttoned socks called *tabi*. These are standard footwear for Japanese traditional clothes and they are cleated, with a separate big toe. One even sees cleated boots on the Japanese street.

Accessories

The two main accessories geiko and maiko carry are traditional paper parasols and silk-covered basket handbags. The parasols are beautiful bamboo constructions with a multi-tude of designs. Handbags are a cornucopia of

Right: Geisha parasols are exquisite bamboo and paper constructs.

Far right: Under umbrellas two Japanese women cross Benkei Bashi bridge in Tokyo. Special *geta* with very high supports are worn, as here, on rainy days and are known as *ashida* or *takageta*. The photograph dates from 1934.

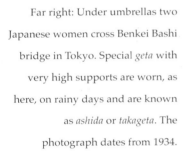

geisha living. There are sheets of *abura torigami*, a traditional paper skin cleanser; a boxwood comb, and a mirror; dance fans, larger than standard; toothpicks, embroidered hand towels, and name cards. Tokyo geisha in the twenties and thirties used to write the initials of their secret lovers on the towels. Almost all Japanese adults exchange name cards in formal situations, but geisha cards are very distinctive. They are prettily designed, often on handmade paper, and contain no contact details.

Geiko and Maiko Spotting

If one is in Kyoto and sees a geiko-maiko pair, they can be distinguished easily. The maiko is by far the more colorful of the two, with many more hairpins and other ornaments; she is the one wearing tall clogs. If still in doubt, check the *obi*; the maiko's hangs down loose almost to her ankles. The geiko's is bundled up in a neat square knot. For checking how long a maiko has been a maiko, a general rule of thumb is the more decorated her kimono, the more junior she is. The *okobo* straps go from red to pink to purple in order of seniority. The *wareshinobu*, the most distinctive hairstyle, belongs to junior maiko.

Right: A maiko, walking on *okobo* clogs to an *ochaya* in Gion. Her *naga-juban* under-kimono is visible as it swings around her ankles.

CHAPTER 6
geisha in the modern world

Permanent change has been a Japanese tradition for over a century and a half now.

Right: Two maiko enjoying the autumn sun in the Gion quarter of Kyoto. They are standing beneath a willow, emblematic of their graceful profession.

Far right: Geisha buying a can of coffee from a vending machine in Gion.

Of course their boss was furious with them. But I couldn't help thinking : when *yakuza* want to get season train tickets, it's the end of the world.

Yugentei Tamasuke, *A Taikomochi's Last Testament*

The venerable male geisha Yugentei Tamasuke beheld some truly outrageous things in his final years, just before the millennium. Gangsters trying to buy season train tickets. Kabuki actors trailing into work with lunchboxes prepared by their "darling wives." Young geisha scolding him in his age, with words like: "Who do you think I am?" He realized with great pain that the sensibility he had grown up in was going to pot. What does saving some money on a season train ticket have to do with *tsu*—for *yakuza*, no less, who should know the score? How is it that the kabuki world, once fabulously decadent, was collapsing under a wave of Anglo-American style domesticity? Why were junior members of the flower-and-willow world so incomprehensibly childish as to tackle him head-on? The proper sense of bearing, the disdain of middle-class mores, and the skillful manipulation of senior-junior relationships were all melting before his appalled gaze.

Changing Times

Postwar Japan has undergone a shift of sensibility as radical as that which gave birth to the geisha profession itself in the mid-eighteenth century. The traditional aesthetics of *iki*, *tsu*, *shibui*, and *wabi* are being buried alive under a wave of *kawaii*—the cute, the naïve. Hello Kitty, cheap and easy, pink and cuddly are in. Formal and debonair, exacting and polished are on the way out. Permanent change has been a Japanese tradition for over a century and a half now. But many observers, domestic and foreign, feel that things have reached a point

where core aspects of the traditional culture are threatened.

Tea ceremony, the linchpin of the Japanese arts, is becoming ever more rule-bound and desiccated. Flower arranging is starting to forget about flowers, abandoning them for bizarre pseudo-sculptures of foam, foil, and plastics. Bored with old-style kabuki theater, audiences are shifting to the newfangled Super Kabuki, a gimmicky derivative featuring flying actors, genuine waterfalls, and lots of other dreary machinery. Japanese archery, an exquisite Zen-based martial art of poise and silences, has suffered the disaster of being adopted into the school sports curriculum. It is now practiced as mere competition, in groups of forty or more, all shouting meaningless greetings at deafening volume as they clatter by each other in the halls. The best of the teachers have long since fled to California. Such are the charges currently being leveled at Japan.

The doyen of foreign polemicists of Japan's "cultural malaise" is Alex Kerr. He is especially scathing about modern Kyoto. "Kyoto hates Kyoto," he writes in his work *Lost Japan*, and goes on to detail the wholesale destruction of the city's traditional architecture, and its replacement with "blah" modern architecture. The temples are lovingly preserved, but taped messages and sponsors' signs disfigure many to the point that Kerr concludes that their custodians no longer fully understand what they are entrusted with.

He develops his critique in *Dogs and Demons: The Fall of Modern Japan*. In its drive for modernization, the country has cast aside much

Many observers feel that things have reached a point where core aspects of the traditional culture are threatened.

of its ultra-sophisticated traditional aesthetics, in everything from textiles to cityscapes. Like many ancient cultures in the modern world, its past is open to the threat of being isolated, theme-parked, and commercialized. "Culture" becomes a jumbled-up mass of "improving" elements imported from anywhere and thrown together anyhow. In particular, the state's emphasis on construction, needed or not, can have disastrous consequences for both country-side and cities. One plan for the historic and beautiful Ponto-cho area was successfully halt-ed by protestors in 1998. The project itself shows how far Kyoto's city fathers have lost sight of their responsibilities for preserving an incomparable heritage:

> [T]he city office [town hall] announced plans for its newest monument—right in the middle of Ponto-cho… The city proposed to demolish a segment in the middle of Ponto-cho and build a new bridge modelled on one that spans the Seine—not even one of the famous old bridges, with picturesque stone arches, but a modern structure of steel girders

Below: Maiko enjoying a backstage chat in Gion. One notice warns fans not to come backstage to interview the performers. The other warns the performers not to leave valu-ables in the changing area.

and tubular concrete pilings of no distinction. To add insult to injury, the city fathers actually proposed to call this copy the *Pont des Arts*. [41]

This grotesque scenario did not come to pass this time around, but Kerr warns that "sooner or later, the old street of Ponto-cho is probably doomed."

Postwar urban planning policy in Kyoto was not a product of the benign neglect of the city's heritage; there was an element of active hostility to the past. In the mid-seventies Iwasaki Mineko inherited the *okiya* she had been brought up in, and decided to make some changes:

> I would renovate the *okiya* and turn part of it into a nightclub!...But then I ran into another roadblock. The house was over a hundred years old so legally ineligible for renovation. Ordinance dictated that we would have to demolish it and start over. [42]

Over a century old, so for the chop. Iwasaki eventually located elsewhere.

By this time, the Japanese economy had been forging ahead for a decade and a half, and was pulling level with Western Europe. By the end of the eighties, it had overtaken them. Old neighborhoods were ripped apart all over the country in the building frenzy that culminated in the bubble economy of the 1980s. Tokyo's Yanagimachi district was among the casualties. By the time the economy soured in 1989, the old Japan was no longer recognizable.

Sooner or later, the old street of Ponto-cho is probably doomed.

In truth, postwar Japan's economic boom was a blessing in extremely thin disguise for most people. Nor were the cultural effects necessarily all as bad as the critics—some of them admitted elitists—insist. In fact, tea ceremony and flower arranging only acquired a mass following for the first time after the war. Perhaps some loss of definition is inevitable under these circumstances. No one is describing the surge in these arts as a renaissance, but at least their future as cultural practices is secure for the time being.

A Dwindling Tradition?

This is not the case, however, for the flower-and-willow world. As early as 1974, Kishii Yoshie (the historian of the Tokyo hanamachi) concluded that the Japanese had lost touch with the shamisen and the sensibility it represented. Writing from the standpoint of a Japanese connoisseur of geisha *asobi*, he pinpointed the break in mentality to 1959, when the Anti-Prostitution Law came into effect. From that point on, the flower-and-willow world became an anachronism.

It turned overnight into a survivor from the age of officially licensed prostitution and legalized indentured service. The government-sanctioned red-light district was the flower-and-willow world's "evil" twin sister, so to speak. Many Japanese of the time saw nothing evil about prostitution, however. The other victim of the 1959 legislation, indentured service, was certainly not mourned by the women of Japan. It presented the flower-and-willow

world with a serious recruiting problem, though.

For all Kishii's regrets, the change in the law was well overdue, and it gained broad social support. There were more factors in play than a decline in traditional sensibilities. The levels of blatant prostitution in the immediate postwar period were shocking in themselves, and an index of how far the once-mighty Japanese Empire had fallen. Magazines and movies covered the harsh lives of the *pan-pan* girls with sympathy. With the state up and running again since 1955, a repeat of the *Maria Luz* incident of 1872 would have been most unwelcome.

The flower-and-willow world bade goodbye to the old dispensation with good grace and mixed emotions. The elite of the profession still had the ear of the powerful. The tradition of politicians marrying geisha or keeping geisha as mistresses continued as before, and still does. *Danna* patronage was now officially banned, but what a geisha did in her private life was now her own business and no one else's, and this tradition continued also. What was about to change more than the flower-and-willow world was the outside world around it.

The pre-war Japanese economy was famous for its huge industrial combines like Mitsubishi

Above: A Tokyo streetscape. Modern Japanese society is rapidly losing touch with the sensibility that formed the geisha profession.

Right: Two geisha in a taxi on the way to work. Geisha sometimes suffer harassment from drunken "salarymen" on the street, so taxis are the preferred mode of transport for most.

Far right: The flower-and-willow world follows current affairs avidly; the people on the pages may well be this evening's guests, especially in the upmarket Kyoto and Tokyo hanamachi. These days, many *ochaya* operate small "home bars;" this seems to be one of them.

and Sumitomo, which dominated the scene. Though broken up during the occupation, they linked up again more loosely through affiliated banks once the Americans had gone home. Their top brass did not suddenly change their leisure patterns in response to military defeat, and they continued to patronize geisha along with the new black market profiteer class, and the more traditional kabuki, *yakuza,* and Buddhist priest clientele. Alongside them were the bosses of hundreds of thousands of small to medium-sized companies, eager to show off their status. Their firms were actually the backbone of the Japanese economy, supporting seventy percent of the workforce.

Paradoxically, two decades of economic growth ground the smaller businesses down, because the shiny new economy was essentially built on their backs. Tens of thousands of these firms were linked up to the major conglomerates as sub-contractors, and the terms dictated to them were draconian. Thousands more were swallowed whole or went out of business. Every time conditions for the big players deteriorated, as in the oil crises of the 1970s, another raft of small firms bade the cruel world goodbye.

The unsung bosses of Watanabe Widgets Ltd. and Kobayashi Grommets, Inc., naturally bade the flower-and-willow world goodbye as well. The survivors, sadder, wiser, and fewer, nervously eyed their expense account budgets. Geisha parties were all very well, but *hana yori dango,* as the saying has it—dumplings come before flowers. There are still small-business chairmen who frequent the hanamachi, but these are just a fraction of the clientele once on tap.

By the 1970s, the old prewar generation was starting to retire. They were increasingly replaced by products of postwar Japan's ferociously competitive education system, corporate samurai who devoted the vast bulk of their waking hours to work. These newcomers had all of the old generation's tenacity, but almost no sense of the old culture of leisure. They preferred to spend their very limited free time in the hostess bars. These were the hanamachi for the average man, open to all, with no stuffy rules and no intimidating rites of etiquette. In place of crooning classical ballads, one could belt out the latest hits on the recently installed karaoke machine. If money was to be burned, it could be done on the golf course; membership fees dwarfed anything charged for *ozashiki* parties. A culture of rather tawdry sophistication spread over Japan like a stain during the 1980s—a panoply of French restaurants, Louis Vuitton handbags, and sake with gold-leaf swirling around in it. Modern was good, and modern meant ignoring or destroying the old. The hanamachi became old men's playgrounds.

Thus the demand side of the equation totters toward the intensive care unit. The supply side is in no better shape. The numbers are unambiguous. From an all-time high of about 80,000 geisha in the mid-1980s, the number has shrunk to less than a tenth of that today. There are currently about 190 geiko and 50 maiko in all of Kyoto. The city's smallest hanamachi, Gion Higashi, has a grand total of five maiko. The trend is not only clear, but accelerating. Maiko are becoming harder and harder to find, and fewer survive the training and decide not

Homogenic

Right: A well-known "geisha" image of the 1990s: the Icelandic pop singer Bjork as a cyber-geisha. The design is a knowing homage/parody blending a number of Asian elements: Thai tribal (neck bands), Imperial Chinese (fingernails), and Chinese ethnic minority (hairstyle). The robe, *obi*, and lipstick are geisha-derived.

to become dedicated geiko. The long *Heisei* recession hasn't helped matters. Every year a slew of *ochaya* close down in each district, and the only question is when the next casualty will follow Yanagibashi into oblivion. The process is cumulative because each hanamachi loses some of its atmosphere as it thins out, fewer customers come, and the ultra-specialized craft workers find their business evaporating. Five *otokosu* dressers and one *mokuroku* poster

painter do not a thriving hanamachi make. Kimono makers are quietly contemplating the collapse of their industry, at the very least for their top of the range.

Some of the reasons for this are entirely positive, just like there are some positive reasons for the much-bewailed state of affairs in tea ceremony and flower arranging. On the whole, and starting from a much lower base, the postwar years have been good ones for women in Japan. Voting rights were extended to all citizens immediately after the war, and gender equality was written into the new constitution. Though it is sometimes honored more in the breach than in the observance, most Japanese people take the egalitarian principles of the constitution very seriously.

Socially, things are much more ambiguous. The glass ceiling is lower and more strongly reinforced, and a "feminist" in Japan means a *man* who opens doors for ladies —like a Western gent from "foggy London." Through the long period of economic boom, Japan somewhat resembled 1950s America. Everybody was expected to end up in a neat little nuclear family, and most Japanese women internalized the model.

This is not to say that a lot of practical feminism on the ground has not been making lots of quiet headway but one thing is clear. Given the opportunity not to join the flower-and-willow world, most women who would have been recruited before 1959 are now declining the privilege.

Below: A constellation of stars: a geiko and maiko holding battledores featuring two idols of contemporary Japan: *Hariipottaa* (left) and *Bekkamu* (right). The battledores are traditional rackets used for family games at the New Year.

Survival Strategies

The result is a serious crisis in the history of the profession. The only comparable scenario is Kyoto after 1868, left high and dry by the emperor's departure for Tokyo. The hanamachi rose very skillfully to the situation then, developing the city's geisha as a brand image and turning the craft into a true profession with its own training institutes.

Public performances, like the Cherry Dances, were instituted to enlist public appreciation and support. They constituted a truly radical departure. Equal imagination and initiative are called for now, but it seems in rather short supply. Stopgap measures are being applied, but no one has come up with a real breakthrough yet. It may be that the circle is impossible to square.

Things look their blackest on the recruitment front. Gion Higashi and Kami Shichiken's advertising campaigns to recruit maiko were a definite nadir in the flower-and-willow world, and the hanamachi have backed away from this approach since 1991. They have subsequently relied on the tried and tired approach of personal introductions through personal contacts. It cannot be said to be working.

For now, the only feasible path to survival is to increase the customer base. Reluctantly and out of sheer need, the *ochaya* are starting to relax their policy of "no new faces." This goes seriously against the grain and it is a risky strategy too, because the old regular client base doesn't like it. They feel that their special position is being usurped, and worry that they won't receive the personalized pampering they are used to once the hanamachi are invaded by the vulgar middle-class hordes. They may well be right, but there is little alternative.

Thus it is that a Japanese businessman armed with nothing more than a platinum credit card can arrive in Kyoto and, with luck, find himself at an *ozashiki* party after some discreet enquiries via his hotel. The hanamachi are going further and putting on parties for whole groups of strangers. One recent special offer was published in a supplement to the December 2002 edition of *Jipangu Club*, the magazine of a senior citizens' group tour body run by Japan Rail West. For a fee of 25,000–30,000 Yen, any member of the public can reserve a place at an *ozashiki* party in one of a rotating series of *ryotei*. This would have been unheard of ten years ago. In Tokyo, Japan

Right: Geisha today retain their traditional roots in the face of constant change in the outside world.

Left: When taken (about fifteen years ago) this photograph would have seemed an incongruous mix of traditional and modern. Now it is the green telephone which seems quaint. Almost all geisha have mobile phones in today's Japan.

Travel Bureau's "Geisha Night Tour" is a some-what cheaper, more foreigner-friendly version. (See Appendix I for details of both). Even more radical is Miyagawa-cho's "geisha-for-a-day" service, which dresses up tourists just like the real thing.

Somehow, the strategy of appealing to a broader clientele doesn't sit well with the flower-and-willow world. But the other option of accepting government aid also has problems. The Foundation for the Promotion of Traditional Artistic Accomplishments (*Ookini Zaidan*) is the flagship of such enterprises. It was set up in 1996 under the auspices of the Kyoto Tourist Association and the Kyoto Association of Hanamachi Unions, with the support of the city government and the Chamber of Commerce. Apart from offering limited financial assistance to individual geisha,

it awards recognition of merit to veteran geiko, in a local version of the Living National Treasure honors scheme. We have already looked at a local government support scheme for geisha in Kanazawa, and noted that a "Faustian pact" was in operation. To get public funds, the hanamachi had to open its rehearsals to the public. A similar deal is in place in Kyoto. The *Ookini Zaidan*'s "Friends program" has a subscription rate of 30,000 Yen per annum. Members can attend a set number of public dance performances. There are also some intro-ductory "how-to" *ozashiki* party events open to non-members.

There is certainly a place for local government support in the overall strategy for the survival of geisha arts and culture. After all, the flower-and-willow world is a major contrib-utor to the local economy. Nowhere more so

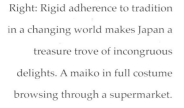

Right: Rigid adherence to tradition in a changing world makes Japan a treasure trove of incongruous delights. A maiko in full costume browsing through a supermarket.

than in Kyoto. The listing of some Kyoto hana-machi for preservation in 1999 is a welcome if belated development. However, excessive reliance on government assistance is bound to dilute the culture of the hanamachi, and compromise its independence and mystique. Even worse, the whole flower-and-willow world may be mummified as some kind of group Living National Treasure. This would be a fate worse than death for a culture of sophisticated play, and the flower-and-willow world has done nothing to deserve it—except survive unchanged from the past. Of all the possible futures for the profession, however, this is the one which seems most likely to come about. The flower-and-willow world will survive, but as a bureaucratized product, a branch of some Ministry of Approved Japanese Fun. Unless, that is, its resources of imagination and innovation get stretched to the limit during the early twenty-first century.

Yet another kind of blind alley is the Asakusa district's fake geisha group, the *Furisode-san* ("The Wide-Sleeves," after their kimonos). The enterprise is run by a company, Furisode Gakuin, which recruits young women, gives them three months dance training, and has them perform at any and all venues for any and all customers. The rates are comparable to real geisha, but the artistry of the *furisode-san* is not. There is something appealingly fresh in their approach, however. "The old system made it difficult for ordinary people to have access to geisha and now the trade is dying," says their manager, Risa Kawai. "The only way to breathe new life into it is to create an environment

where young women will want to carry on the tradition and ordinary people are able to afford their company." [43] They retires its "geisha" at twenty-five; they have to be young and pretty.

One other recent development is the emergence of electronic geisha—literally. A few geisha have gone online and attracted well-deserved attention for their sites. The most noteworthy are the Koito Page, created by a Kyoto geiko, and the *taikomochi* Arai Shozo's brilliantly designed multilingual homepage. The Asakusa hanamachi is also online. (See Internet Resources on page 254 for details).

The International Geisha World

The flower-and-willow world is Japanese through and through. But some foreign faces

Above: A busy maiko eating dinner on the way to an assignment. A napkin protects her precious kimono from stray drops of soy sauce and the like.

Above: Members of the *Furisode-san* performance troupe in action at a Japanese restaurant. These are pseudo-geisha, who undergo three months of dance training and are retired at the age of twenty-five.

have turned up in it over the years, both as inhabitants and (more commonly) guests. By far the best-known non-Japanese geisha is Liza Crihfield Dalby, one of the English-speaking world's great authorities on geishadom. Dalby spent time in Japan as a teenager. She became fluent in the language and practiced the shamisen. Both of these stood her in good stead when she returned to Japan to do the fieldwork for her Ph.D in Anthropology. She chose the Kyoto hanamachi and her subjects there decided that the best way for her to go about things was to become a geisha herself. The results of her research, *Ko-uta: Little Songs of the Geisha World* (1979) and *Geisha* (1983) are the most in-depth academic studies of the topics available in English. She also researched the field of kimonos and has lectured at the University of Chicago.

There have been a small number other foreign geisha, both male and female, as documented by Kishii Yoshie and Yugentei Tamasuke, and detailed in Chapter Two. They mostly seem to have been a product of the White Russian exodus to the Far East following the Bolshevik Revolution. They have gone largely unremembered in the West, however. Unlike Liza Dalby, they left no written records of their lives.

More frequently, foreigners are found as guests in the hanamachi, and the years have seen a string of the great, good, and not-so-good. Charlie Chaplin and the Prince of Wales were visitors in the early decades of the twentieth century; Prince Charles was in Gion Kobu in 1970 (and signed Iwasaki Mineko's favorite fan, much to her disgust). Iwasaki also entertained Queen Elizabeth, though her husband was much more captivated than she with the star geiko. Various hanamachi have hosted Babe Ruth, Sheik Yamani (a fluent Japanese speaker), Jean-Paul Sartre (who was no fun), and a roster of American Presidents including Bush *pere et fils*. Japanese TV recently broadcast a delightful photograph of the youthful Donald Rumsfeld, now American Secretary of Defence, entertaining a giggling geisha. He is pictured propping a chopstick under his nose in a (not quite entirely unsuccessful) impersonation of a New Guinea highlander.

It is still fair to say though, that the bulk of what is interesting in the flower-and-willow world is contained within the Japanese language and is grounded in the traditional Japanese culture.

The traffic has been two-way and a couple of renowned geisha have settled in the United States. Iwasaki Mineko is one and Nakamura Kiharu another. Now eighty-seven, Nakamura was a star of the prewar Shimbashi district, entertained Jean Cocteau, and was an intimate of the then prime minister's younger brother. Tiring of her neighbors' curiosity, she moved to New York in 1956. Iwasaki still awaits the outcome of her case against Arthur Golden. It is apparently close to settlement. And the *Mainichi Shimbun* reports that present-day Asakusa boasts a Japanese-American trainee geisha called Norie.

Conclusion

The single word "geisha" draws around itself a whole constellation of desires and prejudices. For all its hard-headed realism, the flower-and-willow world could not exist without these images. But the geisha world does not belong to anybody. It has carefully threaded its way down the centuries, relying on its image and refusing to play anyone's game but its own. Keeping open house is too demeaning, and being politically correct is too dull. It is above all else a collective of families, almost exclusively female, handing down the craft from generation to generation in an uncharitable world. Whether the world needs the geisha is a question it must answer for itself every evening. This is something it has done since Kiku of Fukagawa first danced 250 years ago.

The picture has not changed much since then, except for the mens' clothes, as they sit

cross-legged on the tatami, drinking, smoking, and bantering. A shamisen strikes up; the geisha and her Younger Sister stand formally arrayed, and hold up their arms to shoulder height. Their embroidered sleeves hang down, to their waists and to their knees. Under their elaborate hairpieces, their faces are expressionless masks of white. The dance begins. The men are now silent. They are looking onto a scene played night after night in the hanamachi—a momentary vision of mortal, human perfection.

Above: Geisha preparing for the New Year in Tokyo. These battledores are of the traditional type. Note the elaborate *pocchiri* clasp on the *obi* braid of the geisha on the left.

APPENDIX I

getting in touch with geisha

Attending an authentic *ozashiki* party is a tall order for the vast majority of Japanese people, let alone for the foreign visitor to Japan. Nevertheless, there are ways to bend if not break the inflexible "no new faces" rule. This is partly because the flower-and-willow world is opening up slightly in response to a decade of recession. Even today, though, the best way to guarantee entrance to an *ozashiki* party remains arriving in Japan as an accredited diplomatic representative or head of state of a foreign country. Or as a senior executive of an overseas corporation doing business with a Japanese company. For ordinary mortals, other humbler options present themselves. For those content to just soak up the atmosphere of the flower-and-willow world, strolling the Kyoto geisha districts around six in the evening is a relaxing way to catch some magical sights.

Many geisha districts in Tokyo and Kyoto have begun to offer performances open to the general public. These are apart from the annual dance performances held in the specialized geisha theaters. The best place for non-Japanese speakers to start is at the tourist information services. A disclaimer at this point: the groups and contact details given below are mostly large, permanent features in the Japanese landscape, but things can change without notice.

The flower-and-willow world is opening up slightly in response to a decade of recession.

Kyoto Tourist Information Centre (TIC) is particularly informative and friendly. It is on the first floor of the Kyoto Tower Building, about five minutes walk north of Kyoto Station. Do not confuse it with the mainly Japanese-language information service right beside the station. They can offer detailed information about upcoming festivals and performances open to the public. It is open from 9:00 to 17:00 on weekdays and from 9:00 to 12:00 on Saturdays, closed on Sundays and holidays. Telephone: +81-(0)75-371-5649.

Both the Kyoto TIC and most major hotels sell tickets for Gion Corner. This is a tourist-oriented revue of traditional Kyoto performance styles, including *kyogen* (noh) comedy, *bunraku* puppet theater, tea ceremony, and dances by geiko and maiko. Shows start at 19:40 and 20:40. The location is Yasaka Kaikan Hall in Gion (Tel: +81-(0)75-561-1119). The season runs from the beginning of March until the end of November.

Two good places to start in Tokyo are: the JNTO Tourist Information Centre, located in the basement of the Tokyo International Forum (Tel: +81-(0)3-3201-3331) and the Asakusa Culture and Sightseeing Centre. It is located one minute's walk from Asakusa subway station, across the street from the landmark

Kaminarimon Gate (Tel: +81-(0)3-3842-5566). The JNTO's opening hours are similar to the Kyoto TIC's; the Asakusa Centre stays open until eight in the evening.

The Asakusa geisha district has an online presence in the form of the Asakusa *geisha to o-tanoshimi kai*, a local geisha arts appreciation society. The site is in Japanese only, at http://www.asakusa-suzuno.com.

In Tokyo, Japan Travel Bureau offers a tour called "Geisha Night," which includes dinner at a *kaiseki* (Japanese haute cuisine) restaurant, and geisha dance and party games. The tour costs 18,000 Yen and includes transport from central Tokyo to a restaurant in the Asakusa district. Tours cater for groups from two to twenty-five people, and reservations can be made at: Tel: +81-(0)3-5620-9500.

*

At time of going to press, Japan Rail West are offering special winter packages in Kyoto. Places at *ozashiki* parties are available on Saturday evenings only in one of a rotating series of *ryotei*. The fee is 25,000–30,000 Yen. Similar packages may be available in other seasons. Reservations can be made (in Japanese) through Kyoto Tourist Association (Tel: +81-(0)75-752-0227) or check with Kyoto TIC.

For the visitor who has always fantasized about becoming a geisha, a fairly recent addition to the Kyoto scene is the "geiko or maiko for a day" service. For a fee of anything from 7,500 to 25,000 Yen, one can visit an *okiya* (geisha house) in the Miyagawa-cho geisha district, and be transformed into a geiko or maiko. The maiko look is more popular and more expensive. The service is mainly availed of by Japanese visitors, so an element of language ability or a Japanese-speaking friend would be advisable. Arrangements can be made through various Japanese travel agents.

Kami Shichiken's beer garden event is an excellent opportunity to meet maiko and geiko informally. It runs all through July and August, at the local *kaburenjo* (geisha dance theater).

Hakone is a popular tourist resort west of Tokyo. The Hakone Geisha Association offers geisha parties which can be booked through one's hotel. The party fee is for a basic unit of ninety minutes, however the exact cost involved depends on numbers of guests, geisha, and other expenses. It will not be cheap.

Finally, visitors and short-term residents should keep an eye out on large department stores in their locality. From time to time they host Kyoto goods fairs, which often feature maiko and geiko dance at no charge.

For those hoping to really sink their teeth into the flower-and-willow world, the prerequisites are residence in Japan, good to excellent Japanese language skills, and a wide network of contacts. The Kyoto Foundation for the Promotion of Traditional Artistic Accomplishments (*Ookini Zaidan*) runs a membership which includes entry to the major Kyoto events (*Kyo-odori*, Dances of the Six Districts, etc.) and other opportunities to attend parties. People with good connections in business or *Nihon buyo* circles should often find themselves within one or two degrees of separation from the flower-and-willow world. Even if you don't fit either bill, there are ways and means. Japan is a circle of circles, and once your friends start asking their friends, and they start asking theirs, the most surprising individuals can turn out to be pure gold for your search. It goes without saying that, in Japan, a pushy attitude will get you nowhere at science-fiction velocities. However much it may offend our modern sensibilities, the flower-and-willow world is an insider's world, and it feels no duty to please strangers. But perseverance is the key, and the journey is always worthwhile.

APPENDIX II

a timeline of geisha and related history

Legendary

The goddess Ama-no-uzume-no-mikoto dances before the Sun
Goddess Amaterasu-no-o-miya-kami, restoring light to the
world.

Yamato and Nara Periods (300AD–794AD)

350: The nucleus of the Japanese state forming in what is now
Nara Prefecture

538–552: The Buddhist religion and Chinese writing system
introduced

Late 600s: Itinerant *saburuko* female singers and dancers active

710: Nara established as capital city

720: *Nihon Shoki* ("Chronicles of Japan") compiled; it contains
the Amaterasu legend

759: The *Manyoshu* ("A Collection of Myriad Leaves")
anthology

Heian Period (794–1185)

794: Kyoto becomes capital city; aristocratic love poetry
develops

900s: *Shirabyoshi* dancer/courtesans emerge; the poet Ono no
Komachi active

c.1000: *The Pillow Book* (Sei Shonagon); *The Tale of Genji* (Murasaki
Shikibu)

1051: Civil war breaks out in northern Honshu

1183: The Minamoto clan takes control of Kyoto

Medieval Period (1185–1467)

1100s–1500s: *Shirabyoshi* dominant as dancers and
entertainers

1185: Shogunate established under Minamoto control

Mid 1180s: Minamoto no Yoshitsune apprehended; origin of the
Shizuka Gozen legend

1191: The monk Eisai introduces Zen Buddhism and tea
ceremony from China

1200s: Tea drinking and Zen Buddhist culture spread among
warrior class

1300s: Ogasawara school of samurai–oriented etiquette
established

1338: Ashikaga family takes control of shogunate

1374: Shogunate begins to officially patronize noh drama

1467: Onin War begins; Kyoto destroyed

**"Warring States" and Azuchi–Momoyama Periods
(1467–1603)**

1480s: Murata Shoko develops the 4 ½-mat tea ceremony space
in the Silver Pavilion

Early 1500s: Noh drama gains a mass following; "Warehouse"
school of tea masters

Mid-1500s: Mizujaya teahouses established in Gion

1587: The warlord Toyotomi Hideyoshi hosts large-scale tea
ceremony in Kyoto

1589: Yanagimachi walled pleasure district established in Kyoto

1590: Hideyoshi unites Japan; early *taikomochi* in existence by
this time; shamisen in use

1592–97: Attacks on Korea; Korean pottery styles introduced

Tokugawa (Edo) Period (1603–1867)

1603: Tokugawa Ieyasu shogun; shogunate moves to Edo; Izumo
no Okuni creates kabuki

1612: First licensed pleasure district opens in Edo

1629: Women banned from performing kabuki

1641: Shimabara licensed district opens in Kyoto; emergence of
tayu and *oiran* courtesans

1647: Commoners banned from performing noh

1652: Kabuki restricted to adult male performers

1657: Yoshiwara licensed district established in Edo

1660s: "Floating world" sensibility begins to develop

1665: *Mizujaya* teahouses formally licensed in Gion

1680s: *Odoriko* dancer/prostitutes become popular

1682: *Adventures of an Amorous Man* (Ihara Saikaku)

1683: The haiku poet Basho begins journey into northern Japan

1703: *Vendetta* by Oishi Kuranosuke forms basis of *Chuushingura*
epic

1712: Teahouses licensed in Ponto–cho

1750: The geisha profession established by Kiku from the
Fukugawa district

1753: Over one hundred Fukagawa *odoriko* consigned to the
Yoshiwara district

1761: Geisha licensed in Yoshiwara

1770s: *Tsu* sensibility develops

1779: First *kemban* established in Yoshiwara

1782–87: Large-scale famine

1798: Inoue School of dance established in Gion

1813: Geisha profession formally licensed in Kyoto

1830s: Fukagawa geisha district overtaken by Yanagibashi (Edo);
Hokusai active

1833–36: Large-scale famine

1843: Fukagawa district disbanded by the authorities

1853: The United States East India Squadron under Perry enters
Edo Bay

1854: The Shimabara licensed district in Kyoto burns down;
Japan formally opened

1856: Townsend Harris in Japan; origin of Okichi and *Madame
Butterfly* traditions

1860s: *Ukiyo–e* prints exported en masse to Europe; dissident
samurai gather in Kyoto

1866–68: Breakdown of shogunate authority

Meiji Period (1868–1912)

1868: Meiji Resroration; Tokyo named capital; geisha-politician
linkage established

1871: Kyoto Exhibition

1872: *Maria Luz* incident; Prostitute and Geisha Emancipation
Act; Cherry Dances begin

1873: Geisha enrolled in training schools

1874: Tokyo geisha rates formally set for the first time; ex–samurai girls becoming geisha

1885: *The Mikado* (Gilbert and Sullivan)

1886: Gion Higashi district breaks off from Gion Kobu

1887: Emperor attends kabuki; the geisha Sadayakko becomes
prime minister's lover

1888: Masked ball at Rokumeikan marks height of
Westernization craze

1894–95: Sino-Japanese War; Tokyo geisha districts coalescing
into their modern form

1900: Sadayakko's theater troupe in Europe; height of *Japonisme*;
c.25,000 geisha in Japan

1902: Morgan-Oyuki courtship

1903: *Madame Butterfly* (Puccini)

1904: Russo-Japanese War

1905: All-Japan Union of Geisha Houses established

1908: Taiwanese geisha active in Nihonbashi

1910: Ainu geisha Pajuro and Gujuro active in Tokyo

Taisho Period (1912–1926)

1914: Japan enters World War I on allied side.

1915: Charlie Chaplin visits Japan and is entertained by geisha

1920s: Three Russian geisha in Asakusa; White Russian and foreign female *taikomochi*

1922: Prince of Wales entertained by geisha at Takamatsu in
Shikoku

1923: Kanto earthquake destroys Tokyo

1924: c.80,000 geisha in Japan

1926: First staging of *Azuma Odori* dances in Shimbashi

Showa Period (prewar) (1926–1945)

1930: Showa Depression begins; geisha deunionize due to falling
rates

1933: First stage production of *The Tale of Genji* banned in
rehearsal for obscenity

1935: Geisha boycott Toho media group

1938: War on China; Nanking massacre

1940: Rationing introduced

1941: Japan enters World War II

1942: Gion Kobu donates two fighter planes to the military

1943: Gion Kobu *Kaburenjo* seized and turned into a munitions
factory

1944: Flower-and-willow world disbanded by government order (March 5)

1945: Tokyo geisha districts obliterated in firebombing; Kyoto districts seriously damaged

Showa Period (postwar) (1945–1989)

1946–47: Geisha districts begin to reform

1948: Shinbashi revives *Azuma Odori*; Cherry Dances recommence

1950: Rationing ended

1952: Yasaka Nyokoba Academy becomes an educational foundation

1957: c. 40,000 geisha active in Japan

1958: *The Barbarian and the Geisha* (John Huston, starring John Wayne and Eiko Ando)

1959: Anti–Prostitution Law in effect; legal *danna* patronage ends; Yoshiwara closes

1960s: Period of high economic growth begins

1964: Gion Kobu internal telephone system established

1974: c.17,000 geisha active in Japan

1982: Kyoto hanamachi advertise for maiko in the mass media for the first time

Heisei Period (1989–present)

1991: Second advertising campaign to recruit maiko conducted

1996: *Ookini Zaidan* established

1997: Crackdown on political wining and dining; *Memoirs of a Geisha* (Arthur Golden)

1999: Yanagibashi district closes; parts of Gion, Miyagawa–cho and KamiShichiken listed.

2000: c. 5,000 geisha of all types in Japan; c.190 geiko and 50 maiko in Kyoto

References

1 John Condon and Keisuke Kurata, *In Search of What's Japanese about Japan*, p.43

2 Aihara Kyoko, *Kyoto maiko to geiko no oku zashiki*, p.119–20

3 Iwasaki Mineko (with Rande Brown), *Geisha, A Life*, p.76–77

4 Ruth Benedict, *The Chrysanthemum and the Sword*, p.177

5 Benedict, op. cit., p.177–8

6 As of July 1999. Statistics for Kyoto geisha and *ochaya* are quoted in Aihara Kyoko, *The World of the Geisha* and Mizobuchi Hiroshi, *Kyoto hanamachi*

7 In *Taikomochi no yuigen* (A Taikomochi's Last Testament) p.34–36

8 For more details on *koken*, see Iwasaki Mineko, *Geisha, A Life*, p.120

9 Mizobuchi Hiroshi, op. cit., p.38

10 See Aihara Kyoko, *Kyoto maiko to geiko no oku zashiki*, p.142

11 See Leslie Downer, *Geisha: The Secret History of a Vanishing World*. Downer's account of the current situation in Tokyo is the most detailed available in English.

12 Leslie Downer op. cit., p.21

13 "My beloved" is the moon.

14 Ruth Benedict, *The Chrysanthemum and the Sword*, p.247–8, quoting Suzuki Daisetz

15 Alex Kerr, *Lost Japan*, p.132

16 Adapted from Aston's translation of *Nihon Shoki* (Chronicles of Japan), in William de Bary (ed.), *Sources of Japanese Tradition*

17 Iwasaki Mineko, *Geisha, A Life*, p.225–226

18 Herbert Plutschow, "An Anthropological Perspective on the Japanese Tea Ceremony," in *Anthropoetics 5*

19 Colin McEvedy's description is of Caesar Augustus, in *The Penguin Atlas of Ancient History*, p.76

20 "Taikomochi Arai Beats Drum on Virtues of Lavish Spending," *Japan Times*, October 13, 2002

21 See, for example, Leslie Downer, op. cit., p.268–269, p.293

22 Haru Matsukata Reischauer, *Samurai and Silk: A Japanese and American Heritage*, p.59

23 Kishii Yoshie, *Onna geisha no jidai* (The Age of the Female Geisha), p.62

24 Statistics for Tokyo up to 1955 are from Kishii.

25 Quoted in *Haru Matsukata Reischauer*, op. cit., p.102

26 Kishii, op. cit., p.109–112

27 Kishii, op. cit., p.89–92

28 François Cellier and Cunningham Bridgeman, *Gilbert and Sullivan and Their Operas*

29 Kishii, op. cit., p.118

30 Quoted in Hashikawa et al., *Nihon no Hyakunen 7: Ajia kaiho no yume*, p.53

31 Yugentei Tamasuke, op. cit., p.14

32 Quoted in Herbert Bix, *Hirohito and the Making of Modern Japan*, p.314

33 See Bix, op. cit., p.490

34 John Dower, *Embracing Defeat: Japan in the Aftermath of World War II*, p.126

35 See Kyoko Aihara, *The World of the Geisha*, p.38.

36 Iwasaki Mineko, *Geisha, A Life*, p.186

37 See Aihara Kyoko, *Kyoto maiko to geiko no oku zashiki*, p.139

38 "Geisha" apparently debuted in written English in an article by Sir E. Arnold in the magazine *Contemporary Review* in 1891, according to the Oxford English Dictionary.

39 The etymology of the word "pongee" shows its popular origin. It comes from the Chinese *benji* ("one's own loom").

40 Iwasaki Mineko, *Geisha, A Life*, p.195

41 Alex Kerr, *Dogs and Demons*, p.187

42 Iwasaki Mineko, *Geisha: A Life*, p.278 (emphasis added)

43 Masako Iijima (Reuters News Agency) "The Gentle Art of the Geisha, Revisited," in the *Globe and Mail*, December 19, 2000

Bibliography

Aihara, Kyoko, *Kyoto maiko to geiko no oku zashiki (Kyoto Maiko and Geiko's Parties)*, Bungei Shunju, 2001

Aihara, Kyoko, *The World of the Geisha*, Charles E.Tuttle and Co., 1999

Baba, Keiichi, *Iki no saho (The Etiquette of Iki)*, Kodansha, 1998

Benedict, Ruth, *The Chrysanthemum and the Sword*, Meridian, 1946

Bix, Herbert, *Hirohito and the Making of Modern Japan*, HarperCollins, 2000

Cellier, François and Bridgeman, Cunningham, *Gilbert and Sullivan and Their Operas*, Little, Brown and Company, 1914

Dower, John *Embracing Defeat: Japan in the Aftermath of World War II*, W.W. Norton and Co., 1999

Downer, Lesley, *Geisha: The Secret History of a Vanishing World*, Headline, 2000

Golden, Arthur, *Memoirs of a Geisha*, New York, Chatto & Windus, 1997

Hashikawa et al., *Nihon no hyakunen 7: Ajia kaiho no yume, (Japan's One Hundred Years 7: The Dream of Asian Liberation; revised edition)*, Chikuma Shobo, 1978

Iijima, Masako, "The Gentle Art of the Geisha, Revisited," in the *Globe and Mail*, December 19, 2000

Iwasaki, Mineko, *Geiko Mineko no hana ikusa: honto no koi wa ippen dosu, (Geiko Mineko's Flower Wars: true love happens only once)*, Kodansha, 2001

Iwasaki, Mineko (with Rande Brown), *Geisha: A Life*, Atria Books, 2002

Kerr, Alex, *Lost Japan*, Lonely Planet Publications, 1996

Kerr, Alex, *Dogs and Demons: The Fall of Modern Japan*, Penguin, 2001

Kishii, Yoshie, *Onna geisha no jidai (The Age of the Female Geisha)*, Seiabo, 1974

Matsukata Reischauer, Haru, *Samurai and Silk: A Japanese and American Heritage*, Charles E.Tuttle and Co., 1987

McEvedy, Colin, *The Penguin Atlas of Ancient History*, Penguin, 1967

Mizobuchi, Hiroshi, *Kyoto Gion*, Mitsumura Suiko Shoin, 1996

Mizobuchi, Hiroshi, *Kyoto Hanamachi*, Mitsumura Suiko Shoin, 2002

Plutschow, Herbert, "An Anthropological Perspective on the Japanese Tea Ceremony," in *Anthropoetics 5*

Uranaka, Taiga, "Taikomochi Beats Drum on Virtues of Lavish Spending"(interview with Arai Shozo) in *Japan Times*, October 13, 2002

West Japan Rail, "Kyo no fuyu no tabi" ("A Winter Trip to the Capital"), supplement to Jipangu Club Magazine, December 2002 edition

Yugentei, Tamasuke, *Taikomochi no yuigon (A Taikomochi's Last Testament)*, Suieisha, 1995

Internet Resources

Caged birds: sister site to Immortal Geisha (see below) concentrating on *oiran* and *tayu* courtesan traditions. Still largely under construction at time of going to press. www.thecagedbirds.com

Hakone Geisha Association: information on geisha entertainment in this popular holiday resort. Helps to arrange geisha parties via hotels. www.geisha.co.jp/eg-01.htm

Immortal Geisha: good-quality site containing photos, articles, and reviews. Partly still under construction. www.immortalgeisha.com

Taikomochi Arai Homepage: a highly informative (and entertaining) multi–lingual site www.mitene.or.jp/~houkan/2002/ejt0210.html

Acknowledgments

This work could not have been written without drawing on many sources, both in English and in Japanese. I am especially indebted to Kyoko Aihara for her *Kyoto maiko to geiko no oku zashiki* and *The World of the Geisha*. For modern Tokyo and Kanazawa, I have drawn on Lesley Downer's *Geisha: The Secret History of a Vanishing World*. Yoshie Kishii's *Onna geisha no jidai* is a wonderfully detailed treasury of Tokyo social life down the years and was greatly helpful. For the *taikomochi* male geisha tradition, I relied especially on the wise and very humorous voice of Tamasuke Yugentei.

It's my great pleasure to thank the friends and acquaintances who answered my queries and directed me to promising materials and sources: Ayako Doi, Akiko Harata (formerly Kofumi), Kayo Hashida, Tsuyoshi (Tsu-san) Inoue, Teiko Iwata, Ikuyo Kataoka, Yukio Katayama, Fumiko Kusume, Ai Tadokoro, Hisako (Chako-chan) Tahara, Junko Uesugi, and Hiroshi Yoshioka at Fish. *Minna-san, taihen o-sewa ni narimashita.*

Arigato also to Martin Howard at PRC Publishing. Heartfelt thanks to Aiko Yoshimoto, who helped enormously with sourcing Japanese materials, and Michael Sharpe, who encouraged me to undertake this project. Finally, thank you and *o-tsukare-sama* to my wife, Yukiko, for her patience and understanding while I was busy writing, and to our daughter Riana, without whom (to quote Ogden Nash) "this book would have been finished in half the time"—but with less than half the fun.

GLOSSARY

asobi: play, both for children and adults

buiki: not *iki*; boorish

bunraku: traditional Japanese puppet theater

danna: a geisha's patron

Edo: Tokyo (historical)

eri: the inside collar of a kimono, at the back of the neck

flower-and-willow world: geisha society as a whole

geiko: a fully qualified geisha (especially in Kyoto)

hanamachi: a geisha district containing *okiya* (geisha houses) and *ochaya* (teahouses)

hangyoku: ("half–jewel") an apprentice Tokyo geisha

hauta: a short song played on the shamisen

Heian: historical period (794–1185)

Heisei: contemporary Japan period

iki: an aesthetic of sophisticated partying associated with the flower-and-willow world

jikata: a geisha specializing in playing music and singing

jimae geiko: an independent geisha who has finished her apprenticeship at an *okiya*

jiuta: ("song of the earth") traditional folk song

kaburenjo: a geisha dance theater and rehearsal space

kemban: the auditing and registration office of a geisha district

kouta: ("little song") a short song accompanied by shamisen

machiai: geisha entertainment rooms formerly popular in Tokyo

maiko: an apprentice Kyoto geisha usually aged between about fifteen and twenty-one

Meiji: historical period (1868–1912) and reigning emperor

minarai: an apprentice maiko

misedashi: a maiko's formal debut

mizuage: the arranged deflowering of a maiko (historical)

mizuage danna: the patron who deflowered a geisha (historical)

mizujaya: the sixteenth-century ancestors of Gion's teahouses (*ochaya*)

nagauta: ("long song") a song accompanied by shamisen

nakai: a professional server at an *ochaya* or *ryotei*

Nihon buyo: traditional Japanese dance

obi: a kimono sash

ochaya: (teahouse) an exclusive function room catering to regular customers only

odoriko: ("dancing girls") entertainers/prostitutes popular in the late 1600s

oiran: Edo courtesan (historical)

okobo: platform clogs worn by maiko

okiya: a house in which Kyoto geiko and maiko live

Ookini Zaidan: Foundation for the Promotion of Traditional Artistic Accomplishments

otokosu: a professional male geisha dresser

ozashiki: a small, private party where guests book geisha to perform in an *ochaya*

pan-pan: street prostitutes during the immediate postwar period

ryotei: a high-class Japanese restaurant

senryu: satirical haiku poem

shamisen (also **samisen**): a three-stringed banjo-like instrument

shikomi: a maid/apprentice

Showa: historical period (1926–1989) and reigning emperor

shirabyoshi: dancers and courtesans popular from the twelfth to the sixteenth centuries

tachikata: a geisha specializing in dance

taikomochi: ("drum-carrier") a male geisha

Taisho: historical period (1912–1926) and reigning emperor

tatami: traditional Japanese flooring, made of thickly woven straw

tayu: Kyoto courtesan (historical)

Tokugawa: historical period (1603–1867) and ruling family

tsu: a masculine form of *iki*

wabi: an aesthetic of restraint and simplicity associated with tea ceremony

wareshinobu: a maiko hairstyle

yakuza: The Japanese Mafia; a Mafioso